Life Long Musings

OR

Fragments Gathered by the Way.

———

A COLLECTION OF POEMS

BY

David E. Dodge.

THE LIGHT, Publishers.
LA CROSSE, WISCONSIN.

Copyright, 1899, by David B. Dodge.

DAVID E. DODGE.

PREFACE.

The productions in this little volume are the result
of a broken and scattered effort through a period of
over forty-five years, most of the time amid the cares
and toils and anxieties necessary in the case of the
poor man to the rearing of a moderately large family. I suspect they contain many imperfections. I
am not sufficiently lettered to judge of their literary
merit: I leave that to the more competent reader.
I expect they will be justly criticised. But if the longings and aspirations and emotions that stirred in my
own being at their writing, shall be awakened by
their perusal in the heart of the reader, my ambition
will be abundantly gratified. Every expression that
would suggest an impure or unholy thought has
been carefully avoided. The glory of God has been
studied, and his grace has enabled me to triumph
over that sordid ambition to introduce for self ad-
advancement that which would simply amuse without elevating and instructing.

Kirwin, Kansas. THE AUTHOR.

Faith's Vision.

PART I.

When Evening round the world had drawn
   Her twilight curtains soft and gray,
I sought the quiet grassy lawn
   To catch the parting kiss of day;
The low west smiled with rosy ray,
   The moon looked down with calm sweet face,
And in the azure far away
   Each glittering star revealed its place.

And as I mused on bygone years,
   On present time and days to come,
On fading hopes and groundless fears
   That mark man's pathway to the tomb,
On superstition's mist and gloom,
   Which oft obscure heaven's holy light,
On nations hastening to their doom
   And souls gone down to endless night;

On avarice and pride and lust,
   Which rule the earth with heavy hand,
On truth low trampled in the dust
   And stern oppression's galling band,
On sin and crime in every land,
   And griefs which mar life's fleeting day,
And evils countless as the sand
   Thick strewn along man's mazy way.

My soul grew sad. How long, how long
Shall Satan triumph? When shall wrong
Give place to right?
Oh, when shall vanish the dark night

That long has brooded o'er the world?
When shall Christ's banner be unfurled
In every land
And love rule all with gentle hand,
 When war and strife shall pass away
And priestcraft lose its blinding sway,
And peace and joy of heavenly birth
Sit smiling o'er the gladdened earth?

Lake Erie's murmur at my feet
   Was soft as infant's evening prayer;
It rose and fell in tones so sweet
   And floated on the evening air;
The moonlight glimmered here and there
   Out on the bosom of the deep;
It was a scene delightful, rare,
   That lulled each troubled thought to sleep.

I dreamed, and softly on my ear
   Sweet accents fell that cheered my breast;
Some spirit seemed to hover near
   And whisper to my soul of rest;
The moon, the stars, the rosy west,
   The lake, all vanished from my sight,
And upward with my heavenly guest
   I soared through space on wings of light.

When, lo, in panoramic view
   I saw the map of time unfold,
Presenting ancient scenes and new
   In characters distinct and bold—
The things of which the prophets told,
   And those by scribes along the way;
And as the lengthened page unrolled,
   My eyes beheld a vast array.

Adam beneath the pleasant shade
   Of Eden sat at height of day,

And by the rippling waters strayed,
   And on earth's grassy carpet lay;

And hand in hand with his fair bride,
   Their spirits knit with love's strong tie,
He roamed the garden by her side
   And drank the love light in her eye;

And gazed upon the earth abroad
   And saw its wondrous beauties blend,
And held communion with his God
   As friend holds converse with his friend;

Exempt from pain and every ill
   And fear of ill in coming days,
He felt his breast with rapture thrill
   And basked his soul in heaven's bright rays.

But oh, how short the social bliss
   And holy joy that filled his life!
As transient as the rosy kiss
   Of morn that bodes the tempest's strife.

The tempter came with subtle art
   And winning smile upon his face,
With pride and malice in his heart,
   And wrought the ruin of our race.

He came to Eve in strange disguise;
   His words in witching accents fell;
The magic of his gleaming eyes
   Enchained his victim with their spell.

Eve listened to the tempter's plea,
   And God's command was soon forgot;
She gazed with longing on the tree,
   Till flown was every filial thought.

Both disobeyed, and quick there came
A sense of guilt and deep distress;
Vainly they thought to hide their shame
In somber shades and fig-leaf dress.

Our parents in their coats of skin,
Badge of their fallen ruined state,
The light of heaven gone out within,
Bemoaned in tears their dismal fate.

And, cursed with noxious weeds and thorns,
The once abounding, fertile soil
Yielded no more its rich returns,
To recompense man for his toil.

Eve saw her folly all too late
As sorrows round her multiplied,
And groaned beneath the crushing weight
Of griefs that did her life betide.

From Eden's bowers they both were driven
To till the ground from whence they came,
And shining cherubim from heaven
Stood by the gate with sword of flame
To guard the way of life's fair tree,
Lest man should eat and live for aye,
Burdened with toil and misery,
Through time's dark night without a ray.

I saw the seasons come and go,
Summer and winter wax and wane,
And scatter blessings here below;
But man sought rest and ease in vain;
For time could never bring again
His former joys, nor griefs assuage,
Nor wipe away the murky stain
That blotted nature's fairest page.

And other woes that wring the heart
    And rend its tender cords in twain,
Their wormwood to the soul impart
    And fill the mind with keenest pain,
Brought by the jealous hand of Cain,
    Were added to their bitter cup;
They mourned the living and the slain,
    Wept o'er the living without hope.

Time's ceaseless moments fled apace,
    Man multiplied and filled the land,
And Nature with abounding grace
    Poured out her gifts at his demand.
I saw his empire wide expand,
    His rising cities stored with gain
Dotting the plains on either hand,
    While other creatures owned his reign.

On rapid wheels the seasons rolled;
As man increased, vice grew more bold;
The human race went far astray,
Walking in sin's delusive way;
Allured by every fleshly lust
They groveled in the very dust,
Till all the earth became defiled,
And each by evil thoughts beguiled
Pressed on forgetful of his God,
Nor dreamed of the avenging rod
That soon was on the world to fall,
In death and darkness shrouding all
Save one small remnant God designed
As the preservers of mankind.

When all the race in merry mood,
Without one thought of coming flood,
Sought pleasure in the various ways
Of business, learning, labor, plays,

Made marriage and bought and sold,
Heaped up their goods and hoarded gold;
Without a sign of danger near
Or aught to wake their slumbering fear,
The earth convulsed with sudden shock
That clove the ground and rent the rock;
As if by some resistless blow
It reeled like drunkard to and fro;

The waters of the mighty deep
Broke o'er their bounds with frantic leap;
The surging waves with deafening roar
Deluged the vales and mountains o'er,
And frowning clouds were tempest-driven
Across the angry face of heaven,
And lightnings gleamed and thunders roared
And rain in ceaseless torrents poured,
Till all the tribes of earth were drowned
But those a sheltering ark had found.

Soon the subsiding waters sped
Back to their native ocean bed,
And Nature spread her carpet new,
Put on her robes of varying hue;
Soon man and beast increased again
And cities rose upon the plain,
While commerce built her busy marts,
And science flourished, and the arts.

But soon the world was filled with strife
And sin and selfishness were rife;
Man's heart was lifted up with pride,
The fear of God was put aside,
Till Sodom in her wild excess
Of rioting and wickedness
Called down stern vengeance from the clouds,
That wrapped her form in fiery shrouds,

And buried her beneath the waves,
And hollowed out the watery graves
Of other towns less vile than she
Beneath the dark and sullen sea.

I heard the bondman's bitter groan
Beside the Nile, and plaintive moan
Of mothers weeping o'er their dead,
With breaking heart and drooping head.
And saw the toiler 'neath his load
Urged on by cruel lash and goad,
With none to comfort, none to cheer,
Through all the slowly dragging year,
Till Moses came at God's command,
With shepherd's staff in outstretched hand,
And smote the land with stunning blow
And laid its pomp and glory low,
And set the groaning captives free
And led them through the parted sea.

Though by the cloudy pillar led
And on the food of angels fed,
Though drinking water from the rock
That flowed for man and herd and flock,
Though God his mighty power displayed
In awful majesty arrayed,
Proclaimed his law in thunders loud
Mid flaming fire and smoking cloud,
Yet from his ways they walked apart
With stiffened neck and hardened heart,
Ran on in sin's deceptive path
Till in the fierceness of his wrath
He swore they should not find his rest,
But perish in the wilderness.

And when at last the tribes possessed
    The goodly land to Abraham given,

With all the stores of nature blest
    And lighted with the smile of heaven,
How soon from God their footsteps strayed
And all their loyalty decayed!
Blinded by sin they soon forgot
His benefit, and scrupled not
To worship gods their hands had made,
On lofty hills, in leafy shade,
Or with their forms in reverence bent
Adore the starry firmament,
Or bow before the golden calves
Set up at Bethel and at Dan;
Dark superstition's willing slaves,
They after every error ran.

O Israel!   What hast thou done?
Thy ways procured thy fearful doom;
I saw the setting of thy sun,
Which left thee wrapped in midnight gloom;
The Assyrian king thy pride abased,
And laid thy goodly cities waste;

Thy failing strength'could not avail
    To stay the mighty conqueror's hand;
I heard thy captive daughters wail
    Disconsolate in distant land;
Thy moon has waned, thy stars have set,
    No remnant of thy tribes appears,
Or, if perchance it lingers yet,
    Is shrouded in the mist of years.

I saw the Assyrian empire rise
A giant towering to the skies,
Of massive bulk and robust form,
Of iron grip and brawny arm,
With sturdy limb and calloused heel
And muscles firm as cords of steel,

Of visage grim and manners rude
And restless passions unsubdued.

He grasped the sword with bloody hand,
Spread death and terror through the land,
Applied the torch with fiendish smile
That lit the glaring funeral pile
Of cities humbled in the dust,
Fainting before his savage thrust;
Unskilled to stay the evil hour,
They sank beneath his crushing power;
Their glory crumbled, and their might,
Their day went out in rayless night.

The nations trembled at his tread,
And kings grew pale and armies fled,
Or, on the bloody battlefield
Mid clanging sword and spear and shield,
Laid down in ghastly death's embrace
With gapping wounds and pallid face,
Or, exiled from their native land,
Were led afar a captive band,
In fetters strong and clanking chain,
To grace the mighty conqueror's train,
And groan beneath the iron rod
And tremble at the oppressor's nod.

And peaceful homes where plenty smiled
And love the passing hours beguiled,
Where housewife sang and children played
And husband well contented stayed,
Save when his duty called him thence
For honest toil or home's defence,
Were desolated, overthrown,
The children wandering sad and lone,
The mother ravished, stark and dead,
The father on his gory bed,

A prey to savage bird and beast
That fought around the bloody feast.

He worshiped gods of Lust and Pride,
Bade modest Virtue stand aside;
And Prostitution, brazen faced,
Of wanton looks and acts unchaste,
Was crowned with honors and admired;
And rites unclean, by her inspired,
Corrupted peasant, priest and king,
And poisoned love's pure genial spring.

I saw his mighty power decay
And all his glory pass away;
Saw Nineveh's strong wall come down,
Her gilded temples overthrown,
Her palaces, where pride and lust
Once reveled, prostrate in the dust.
Her flaunting banners wave no more
Above the foe mid battle's roar;
No armed bands parade her streets
Proclaiming bloody battle feats,
Nor jumping chariots, prancing steeds;
No heralding of daring deeds
Shall from her crumbled walls resound;
Her nobles slumber neath the ground;
Her thronging multitudes have fled
And left her with her sleeping dead.

As Nineveh sank to decay,
    No more to lift her haughty head,
Chaldea ruled with wider sway,
    And forth her conquering armies sped,
With flashing sword and glittering spear
And standards waving in the air,
With thundering tramp and rumbling wheels
And shoutings loud and trumpet peals,

And horses snorting for the fray—
A mighty host in dread array.
The nations heard the sound afar,
Beheld the gathering cloud of war,
And on its foldings read their doom—
A ravished country, ruined home.

Lady of Kingdoms, Babylon stood
Spanning Euphrates' turbid flood:
Her brazen gates and massive walls
And hanging gardens rich and fair,
Her gilded palaces and halls
And temples towering in the air,
Brought her renown; her king, in pride,
Boasted his power, and God defied.

His conquering troops by fire and sword
    Spread desolation far and near;
The nations fainted at his word
    And cities stood aghast with fear;
His cohorts tramped along the Nile
And Egypt sank in deadly swoon;
Pharaoh with broken arms the while
Bewailed his wounds with bitter groan.
With sateless greed the savage host
Invaded Palestina's coast,
And Tyrus, mistress of the sea,
Too proud to bend the suppliant knee,
Too weak the onset to withstand,
Beneath the strong invader's hand
Sank like a stone cast in the deep
Down to her silent dreamless sleep,
Nor waked till seventy years had flown,
And Babylon's power was overthrown.
And other cities felt the shock
That made their strong foundations rock
And topple to their overthrow,
Powerless to stay the conquering foe.

And Judah, broken and distressed,
By heavy weight of sin oppressed,
His holy city desolate,
The Temple ruined, mourned too late
The hidings of Jehovah's face,
Who drove him from his native place,
In distant lands to groan and sigh
And pine beneath a foreign sky.

While sounds of revelry were heard
  In proud Belshazzar's festive hall,
The fingers of a hand appeared
  And wrote his sentence on the wall.
The God of heaven was honored not,
  But mid the revels wild and high,
The vessels of His house were brought
  To heighten still the revelry.
That very night the king was slain;
  His mighty empire passed away;
The monuments that yet remain
  Are slowly mouldering to decay.

And then the Beast that Daniel saw,
Of ugly form and sateless maw,
Strode up and down with open mouth;
Nor could the desert parched with drouth,
Nor swollen stream with rushing tide,
Nor rugged steeps of mountain side,
Nor weary stretch of wilderness,
Make his voracious instincts less.

Chaldea, crushed beneath his paw,
  Wounded and bleeding, helpless lay;
His conquering march the people saw,
  And trembled, crouching in dismay;
He crunched the kingdoms piece by piece,
  The spoils of many cities won,

Invaded Egypt, Syria, Greece,
　Till on the field of Marathon,
With broken teeth and wounded cheek
　He cowed before the impetuous Greek.

Though checked he fainted not, but still
Brought princes subject to his will,
And ruled till the prophetic hour,
When Alexander broke his power.

I saw the winged Leopard fly,
And caught the fierce glance of his eye
As from his native lair he sped;
By Granicus I saw the dead,
Satrap and servant side by side
Their warm blood mingling with the tide;
I heard the shout of victory
And saw the Persian horsemen flee,
The mercenaries heap on heap
Lie down in their last, dreamless sleep.

Gathered two hosts in fierce array
Where the Pinarus wends its way,
Advanced with ringing battle cries,
Their pœans echoing to the skies:
I heard their weapon's savage clank
Along the river's muddy bank,
Where Greek met Greek in tumult wild,
Till all the ground with dead was piled.
I heard the wounded soldier sigh
　For wife and child and native hearth,
As closed in death his languid eye,
　Forever sealed to scenes of earth.

A wail arose along the shore
As Tyrus sank to rise no more,
Her pride gone down to ocean caves:
No more her white sails deck the waves;

No more her hardy mariners
Lade gallant ship with costly wares;
With trade no more her streets resound,
But o'er them silence broods profound;
Where massive buildings once have been,
The fisherman now spreads his seine.

On broad Arbela's battle plain,
Three hundred thousand warriors slain
Enriched the soil with human gore;
I saw the crimson current pour
From severed limb and gaping wound;
And heard the strange, tumultuous sound
Of mingled tongues in loud commands,
Urging with oaths the faltering bands.

How did the stoutest hearted cower
Before proud Rome's resistless power,
As vanquished tribes were made to feel
The pressure of her iron heel!
Empires were humbled at her feet,
Powerless the savage foe to meet.
On Grecian soil her armies trod,
Polluted Judah's sacred sod,
On verdant isles and Afric's shore,
Resounded oft the battle's roar,
And Europe owned her mighty sway,
And prostrate powers in suppliance lay.

Her eagles hovered in the air,
Her conquering legions knew no fear;
In distant climes, on land and sea,
Her warriors fought triumphantly,
And piled the field with gory dead,
And bands of vanquished captives led,
To swell the triumph as they strode
In marshal pomp the homeward road.

In scenes of deadly strife and blood,
Before the gazing multitude,
With furious beasts impelled by rage,
I saw these captive souls engage
In the arena, while the sound
Of loud applause went round and round.

O Hannibal! thine oath was vain,
Thine arm too feeble to maintain
Supremacy; of no avail
Thy skill; thou strugglest but to fail.
Thou could'st not stay the whelming tide
That swept the city of thy pride;
Her walls went down with thundering jar;
Her dying groan was heard afar.
How was thy soul with sorrow wrung!
Thy breast with bitter anguish stung,
Till life thou gladly did'st give up,
Drain with thy lips the deadly cup!

PART II.

The day drew near for man's release
    From sin and Satan's fatal power;
Bright angel bands, proclaiming peace,
    Hailed with delight its opening hour.

The nations knew a transient rest,
    The clang of noisy war had ceased,
With wholesome laws the land was blest,
Learning and civil arts increased.

With rapt attention man beheld
    The signs of the approaching light,
And hope in longing hearts upwelled
    And gleamed across the murky nig

The promised Seed at length appeared
  To bruise the Serpent 'neath his feet,
O'erthrow the kingdom he had reared,
  And man's deliverance complete.

I saw a Babe in manger born,
  Reared up in humble poverty,
To feel contumely and scorn,
  That he a captive world might free.

The man of sorrows, Diety
  Veiled in the flesh, beneath the load
Of the world's sin, in agony,
  Sweat drops of his own precious blood.

Betrayed, deserted by his friends,
  Mocked by the jeering multitude,
Bearing the strokes of cruel hands,
  Before the Jews he humbly stood,

To bear their taunts inspired by hate
  And envy armed with base deceit,
While Justice powerless to abate
  Their zeal, lay trampled 'neath their feet;

To Pilate's judgment hall was led,
  By soldiers hailed on bended knee;
With crown of thorns upon his head,
  They bowed and worshiped feignedly.

Rent by the nails, his quivering form
  Was fastened to the rugged tree;
And trickled down the life stream warm
  To pay sin's fearful penalty.

Our substitute, he thus was slain,
  His blood poured out for fallen man,
To wash away guilt's murky stain
  And win us back to God again.

His flesh imprisoned in the tomb,
　Hope fled away on weary wing,
Till life's return dispelled the gloom
　And raised him up a conquering king.

Hell's triumph short, to him was given
　To compass all his foes defeat,
Resume his princely place in heaven
　And make his victory complete.

　His followers in joy renewed
　　Went forth in his almighty name,
　With power and zeal from heaven endued,
　　The joyful tidings to proclaim.

The hand of Persecution red
With blood of martyrs freely shed
Sought by devices born of hell
Christ's valiant soldiers to repell.
The gleaming sword with swift descent,
The frantic mob on murder bent,
The cruel stocks, the prison gloom,
And savage threats of coming doom,
Were all employed to check the tide
That rose and spread on every side.

The more 'twas sought to stop its flow,
The more it seemed to spread and grow,
Till wide its healing waters pure
To sin-sick souls brought hope and cure.
The fiery fagot burned in vain;
Naught could the Christian's zeal restrain;
Put to the rack, asunder sawn,
Through thronged streets in rudeness drawn,
He faltered not, but firm in death,
Exulted to his latest breath.
As perished one, another rose
Undaunted by his murderous foes.

Yet in the dens and caves of earth,
 In lonely mountains wild and drear,
Afar from home and place of birth,
 And all that loving hearts hold dear,

Some safety sought from tyrant's power
 Who fain would check the widening leaven,
And passed away each long-drawn hour
 In prayer and thoughts of home and heaven.

Hungry and clad in coats of skin,
 Hated by all save of their kind,
But hating not, though loathing sin,
 To deeds of mercy they inclined.

With fiendish rage, Persia and Rome
 Besmeared their hands with human gore,
Destroyed many a happy home
 Where love and pleasure dwelt before.

Nero, urged on by bitter hate
 That could not Christian zeal abide,
That seas of blood failed to abate,
 Spread death and desolation wide.

And others following in his path,
 With spite and envy all aflame,
In cruel deeds vented their wrath
 On all who bore the Savior's name.

Yet these poor victims dauntless stood
 Amid the storm that round them rolled,
Or bravely stemmed the dashing flood
 With faith unshaken, calm and bold.

Tormented, crushed, consumed by fire,
 Slain with the sword, to beasts of prey,
Sustained by hope and strong desire,
 They turned not from the narrow way.

In Persia multitudes were slain
  By Sapo, monarch of that realm;
Not fear of death nor torturing pain
  Their steadfast faith could overwhelm.

Mid persecutions fierce and long
  That trampled thousands in the dust,
Vigor-endued, the church grew strong
  And onward pressed, in God her trust.

Till thrones and empires owned her sway,
  And peoples bowed at her behest,
When passed her former state away;
  The oppressor she, not the oppressed.

Eager for gain, inspired by lust,
  Greedy of power, puffed up with pride,
In wealth and might she made her trust,
  And life divine within her died.

I saw the Whore of Babylon sit
  Upon the Beast of scarlet hue,
The nations crouching at her feet
  With fear and homage only due

To Him who built yon starry dome,
  And guides through space this whirling ball,
Pours out his grace on all who come
  And for his love and mercy call.

Her form in gorgeous robes arrayed,
  Bedecked with costly gems and gold,
A name of mystery on her head,
  Her looks and actions lewd and bold;

Drunken with blood, debauched and vile,
  She held her cup of filthiness,
With jeweled hand and wanton smile,
  To all who would her charms confess.

With empty forms and senseless rites,
　That could no saving grace impart,
With pageantry and fancy's flights,
　She sought to captivate man's heart.

Only a remnant true to God,
　By persecution sorely tried,
Scattered in various lands abroad,
　Were bold to dash her cup aside.

And moral darkness dense, profound,
　Save here and there a glimmering ray,
Brooded o'er earth, while Satan bound
　With stronger bands his willing prey.

Kings trembled and obeyed her nod,
　And crouched in terror at her feet;
Claiming to rule in place of God,
　She sought o'er earth a sway complete.

Nor dared but few to lift their voice
　Against her arrogance, and claim
Of universal rule, no choice
　But to submit, passive and tame.

She set a price on crime, for gold,
　Of wickedness a traffic made,
License for various sins were sold,
　As men sell articles of trade.

And, when revolting from her sway,
　One dared to lift his puny form,
How soon in helplessness he lay
　Beneath her feet, crushed like a worm!

Willing to curse, but loth to bless,
　Ready to kill, but slow to save,
An enemy of righteousness,
　Ever insatiate as the grave,

Her minions like a hungry swarm
  Of locusts quite devoured the land,
Poured out in streams the life blood warm
  Of hated foes at her command.

In Alpine valleys when the snow
  Lay white and cold on mountain side,
Whole neighborhoods pressed by the foe,
  In self defense lay down and died.

While others fled in exile bands,
  Rather than yield their liberty
To walk as Holy Writ commands,
  From rule of priestly tyrants free;

And sought to find a hiding place
  From cruel hands that pressed them sore,
Where they might worship God in peace,
  Nor feel again the oppressor's power;

But sought in vain: the watchful eye
  Of jealous clerics scanned the world,
If it in some hid spot might spy
  Where Liberty her flag unfurled.

In Constance, officers of state,
Clergy and nobles famed and great,
In council met to see which name
Of three contending popes might claim
The honor of this title proud
O'er which they wrangled long and loud.
But some more mindful in their zeal
That heretics their power might feel,
Labored with fiendish hate and rage
That did their utmost skill engage,
Like demons from the pit let loose,
To crush an honest priest, John Huss,
Till they secured his overthrow

And laid his hopes and prospects low.
I saw him at the fiery stake,
A prisoner bound for Jesus' sake,
In hateful garb; I heard his prayer,
And saw the crowds in wonder stare
As calmly mid the scorching flame
He called on God in Jesus' name
And passed triumphantly away
To bask in heaven's eternal day.

Jerome of Prague, bound and oppressed
Through schemes unjust, in vain sought rest
From galling chains and prison gloom,
But pined afar from friends and home.
And cunning foes with hellish spite,
By craft and guile with fierce delight,
Sought by devices dark and dire,
With hate that glowed like flaming fire,
To sate their vengeance by his death;
Nor could they rest till his last breath
Expired beneath the cruel stroke
And vanished mid the flame and smoke.

John Ziska with his frantic horde
Of followers, by fire and sword
Left desolation in his path;
His soul aflame with vengeful wrath,
With deeds of cruelty, and blood
Thought to avenge the cause of God,
Advance Messiah's rule and swell
The triumphs of Emanuel;
But by his barbarous dealings proved
His heart from Jesus far removed;
And, crushed by civil strife and war,
Bohemia's wail was heard afar.

O mournful sight, Calabria!
What pen can paint the scene I saw,

When persecution's crushing blow
In death thy loyal sons laid low?
A fiend, reckless of human life,
Held in his hand a bloody knife,
Then to the martyr's throat applied
The sharpened steel, and the red tide
From severed vein came gushing, warm,
As sank in death the victim's form.
The dead were piled a ghastly heap;
I saw spectators turn and weep
As, victims of a priestly hate,
These martyrs met their dreadful fate.

O Spain! how skillful was thy hand
To banish freedom from thy land,
And forge the chains that held secure
The vassal neath the tyrant's power!
Supported by the church and state,
Upheld by laws thou didst create,
The Inquisition, leagued with hell,
Performed its bloody labors well;
By sword and dungeon, rack and fire,
Led on by hate and strong desire,
Inflicted pains and griefs untold
To gain the tortured victim's gold;
Spread death and desolation wide
O'er valley's green and mountain side;
Banished from native land and home,
In exile other lands to roam,
Alike the Christian, Jew and Moor,
The high and low, the rich and poor.

When heretics, in strange array,
Marched to the dread auto-da-fe,
Thronged by the jostling multitude,
Mid taunts and jeerings harsh and rude,
Rulers and nobles gathered there,

Delighting each his part to bear.
I see e'en now in fancy's eye
The wretched victim passing by,
With the corosa on his head,
And pictured flames, by devil's fed,
On sanbenito round him cast:
And when I see his form at last
Writhing and shrinking in the fire,
As the hot flames mount high and higher,
I start aghast and ask to know
What dragged the human soul so low,
That lowest fiend of darkest guise
Could not worse cruelty devise.

I saw the blood in torrents flow,
The masses surging to and fro,
And heard the rush of hurrying feet
Along the blood-besprinkled street,
As France, impelled by frantic rage,
Was making time's most bloody page.
And as the mind turns in review
Of that dark day, Bartholemew,
It starts aback with deep recoil
And wonders at the sad turmoil,
And hate and strife and bigotry,
That bade sweet Peace in terror flee;
And why, where once the cheering light
Of Christ had banished pagan night,
That there should be such wide remove
From Him whose name and deeds are love.

In Piedmont valleys bright and green,
My eyes beheld a mournful scene:
Homes disappeared 'mid flame and smoke
Beneath the cruel tyrant's stroke;
Where once went on the busy round
Of cheerful toil, I heard the sound

Of lamentations on the air,
The ruffian's shout, the Christian's prayer,
The noise of conflict and the groan
Of wounded left to die alone,
Of women weeping o'er the slain,
Striving to call back life again,
The cry of babe from mother torn,
And tempted maiden's bitter scorn;
And saw the exiles in their flight
Across the mountain's rocky height,
Hastening to lands before unknown,
Hearts rent with longings for their own.

The British Isles with faction rent,
Each sect on other's ruin bent,
Endured the horrors of that strife
That views as nothing, human life
When standing in the bigot's way;
Nor cares for liberty's decay,
But seeks to overthrow and crush
All human rights, to quickly hush
The faintest murmur of complaint;
And those in power, without restraint,
As turned to them the favoring tide,
Each eagerly with other vied
In deeds of barbarous cruelty
That devils might rejoice to see.
Papist and Protestant alike,
With lifted arm ready to strike,
Watched for the favored time to smite
With savage blow the opponent's might.

Henry, "Defender of the Faith,"
Causing to tremble at his wrath
The slaves that waited for his beck,
Brooked no control that sought to check
The fervor of his pious zeal.

Without a thought of other's weal
He trod on every human right,
His scepter swayed with fierce delight;
And streams of blood that failed to sate
His burning thirst or quench his hate
Flowed through the land; and martyr fires
Only increased his base desires.

The "Bloody Mary's" cruel reign
Was marked by many a crimson stain;
Often the fiery fagot glowed,
And dark grew many a bright abode,
As man and wife asunder torn,
Of all domestic pleasure shorn,
Pined in the gloomy prison cell.
The human tongue is weak to tell
The pains and horrors there endured,
As captive, in the gloom immured,
Was tempted, tortured and distressed,
Without a hope to cheer his breast
But the one hope—a life of bliss—
If faithful to the end in this.

Her sister, too, the "Good Queen Bess"—
A title mild—was none the less
A cruel princess, and the crimes—
With due allowance for the times—
Were still the promptings of a heart
Selfish and hard in every part;
Or by some pressure overborne,
Or held by oath that she had sworn,
She yielded to the subtle plea
Set forth so oft—expediency—
And stained her hands with blood of those,
Who in her fear she counted foes,
Because of something in their creed,
But not for wicked word or deed.

In Portugal and Germany,
    In southern clime and northern state,
In other lands beyond the sea,
    Mankind seemed borne away by hate.

I saw Joan of Kent embrace
    With courage firm the martyr's death,
Nor could discern a single trace
    Of wavering to her latest breath.

And others, too, as firm as she
    Endure the flames for conscience's sake;
Though bound the flesh, the soul was free,
    And gloried, buoyant, at the stake.

Calm was the death of Mary Dyer;
    I heard her glory in the Cross;
Her soul aglow with heavenly fire,
    She counted earthly life but dross.

The senses sicken at the scene,
    The mind recoils, the heart grows faint:
How oft the lowly Nazarene
    Suffered in some poor, humble saint!

I saw in loved America
The toiling slave, and heard him pray
For his release, but long in vain
Before was rent the galling chain.
I saw the wife from husband torn,
And infant from its mother borne,
Purchased by stranger, as one buys
His neighbor's beast or merchandise,
With haggling o'er the price, while she
Stretched out her arms imploringly,
Or wrung her hands in blank dismay
As scalding tear drops traced their way
From pleading eyes whose look alone
Might break and melt a heart of stone.

To base and carnal lust a prey,
I saw sweet virtue's flower decay
Like blossom seared by autumn frost,
Its beauty gone, its fragrance lost.

I saw the driver's arm extend,
And then the cruel lash descend
On naked form and quivering flesh,
Till gushed the life blood warm and fresh
And stained the hand that gave the blow,
And trickled down in crimson flow.
Of every human right despoiled,
Year after year the bondman toiled,
I heard his groan for liberty,
And saw his struggles to be free;
But when he strove for his release
It only made his toils increase,
Till in fulfillment of his plans
God smote the shackles from his hands.

And as the whole my eye surveyed,
In every land I saw portrayed
Tumults, commotions, strife and war,
Shedding their baneful influence far,
Theft, slander, murder, deeds of lust,
Hate, envy, jealousy, mistrust,
Fanaticism, bigotry
That fails another's right to see,
Idolatry and rites unclean,
And acts debasing and obscene,
Deceit and vanity and pride,
And all the ills that earth betide.

My sense grew weary to behold,
  And turned away in blank despair,
As to my view time's map unrolled
  And showed the past all pictured there—

Sad scenes that make the heart grow faint,
　Congeal the veins with icy chill,
Sadder than human hand can paint,
　Making the soul with horror thrill,
Marring the page to present time
　With every form and shade of crime.

Turning to him, my guide, I said:
　"How long shall this sad state prevail?
Has white-winged peace forever fled?
　Shall God's eternal purpose fail,
That Christ shall trample 'neath his feet
　The wily serpent's hydra head,
Confound his pride and vain conceit,
　And lay his hopes of triumph dead?

"Shall cruel war forever wage,
　And human blood forever flow?
Is there no coming peaceful age
　That naught of strife and hate shall know?
Shall man forever be the dupe
　Of man more cunning than himself?
Forever 'neath the burden stoop
　Imposed by heartless greed of pelf?

"Shall lust, debasing and unclean,
　Defile the earth forever more?
Will never cease the bustling scene
　Or vain ambition's strife for power?
Shall appetite forever sway
　And drag man downward to the ditch,
Till all his nobler powers decay,
　And he sinks down a hapless wretch?

"Will priest craft never cease to bind
　The human soul with galling chains,
Obscure with gloomy mists the mind
　Till only glimmering light remains?

And gloat and glory o'er the spoil,
  Wrung from the wildered devotee,
Who, though oppressed with ceaseless toil,
  Fails not to offer up his fee?

"Must pestilence in darkness walk,
  And grim destruction waste by day,
Gaunt, famine-like a specter stalk,
  To curse this bright, green earth for aye?
Must dire disease forever be
  A scourge to chasten human kind?
The world from plague be never free,
  And man exemption never find?"

He answered me with words of cheer:
  "God's purposes shall never fail;
Let faith dispel your every fear,
  For Judah's lion shall prevail;
Nor know discouragement till he
  Has judgment set in every land,
And all the islands of the sea
  Have yielded to his mild command."

PART III.

I turned again and all had changed,
  The past had vanished from my view,
On fairest scenes my vision ranged,
  And everything seemed made anew:
I saw the smile that love begets
  Wreathing the radiant human face,
Heard no sad murmurings and regrets,
  But words of tenderness and grace.

I looked; no arsenals and forts,
  No march of armies could I see,
No rendezvous where man resorts
  To learn war's savage cruelty.

No flaunting banners to be seen,
 No martial pomp and blazonry,
No mighty warships plowed the main
 And frowned defiance o'er the sea.

The sword had crumbled into dust,
 Or been transformed to plowman's share;
Wielded no more with deadly thrust,
 To pruning hook had turned the spear:
The various implements of strife,
 New-shaped to implements of peace,
Tended to lengthen human life
 And human happiness increase.

My native land, in smiling green,
 Lay clothed in nature's fairest dress,
Her mountains, and her vales between,
 Presented scenes of loveliness;
Though marred before by man's device,
 And deeply stained and marked by sin,
For her one paid redemption's price,
 And purged and made her borders clean.

There stood no gaudy temples there
 Adorned with carvings rich and gay,
Frescoed and stained with costly care,
 Built less for worship than display,
Where fashion's follower, inspired
 By restless longing, seem to ween
That all of life to be desired
 Or coveted, is to be seen.

No courts where Justice hangs her head
 And Wrong presides with cunning mien,
Where Falsehood grins and Truth has fled
 And Fraud sits smiling and serene;
Where juries moved by prejudice,
 Or wrought upon by skillful plea

Arranged so dext'rously and nice,
  The real issue fail to see.

Along the street, with haughty air,
  I saw no pompous cleric stride,
Gaily attired with choicest care,
  Puffed up with vanity and pride,
Who feeds his flock, famished and faint,
  On food that can no strength impart,
Insipid to the hungry saint,
  Unsavory to the longing heart.

I heard no clamoring for divorce,
  For Lust had fled and Love was queen,
And ruled with strong, but gentle force,
  And banished all that came between
Two wedded hearts, and Jealousy,
    Green eyed with rage, had found her death
And each from bubbling passions free
    Breathed deep of Love's inspiring breath.

No more was seen the vile saloon
  Where debauchees hold revelry
Early and late at night and noon,
  Reckless of home's deep misery,
Forgetful of the sighs and tears,
  The broken heart and ruined hope,
The anguish of distracting fears,
  That swallows every pleasure up.

No brothel where the slave of lust
  Is like the ox to slaughter led,
And wallows in the very dust
  And holds communion with the dead—
Those dead to all that's good and pure,
  Whose poison cup like magic spell
All potent sparkles, but to lure
  Their victims to the depths of hell.

No gambling hells to tempt the young
  With promise fair of speedy gains,
Where human fiends with oily tongue
  Addle each new adventurer's brains,
Till like a helmless ship at sea,
  Tossed by the storm that madly raves,
He drifts and finds no sheltering lee,
  But dashes on the angry waves.

The theater, where foolish plays
  Attract the gazing multitude,
Where Vice but half conceals her ways,
  And Wantonness stands almost nude,
Had disappeared. The festive hall
  Where social revelry runs high,
And mirth and music lead the ball
  Till morning light, met not my eye.

No demagogue, inspired by greed
  And vanity, found there a place,
Where he the listening throng could lead
  With noisy speech and brazen face,
Possessed of wondrous skill and tact
  To deal in craft and sophistry,
Make wrong look right and white look black,
  Injustice seem like equity.

On city street, by country side,
  For worship to Almighty God,
Apart from ostentatious pride,
  Many a modest chapel stood,
Where praise ascended day by day
  Like incense to the throne above,
And brightly shone the Spirit's ray,
  And all was harmony and love.

I looked, and, lo, in other lands
  The former things had passed away;

Cold northern plains and southern sands
  Rejoiced to own Messiah's sway;
Praises came floating from the wilds;
  I heard the mountain dwellers sing;
And songs arose from distant isles;
  And all were glad, for Christ was king.

No more on Ganges' turbid wave
  The Hindoo mother cast her child,
Thinking by this sad act to save
  Her soul, by sin's dark stain defiled,
Nor lingered Superstition's slave,
  While fainter grew his parting breath
That he his wasted form might lave.
  Mid the expiring throes of death.

No pilgrimage to distant shrines,
  Where conscience-smitten souls resort,
And men of craft and base designs,
  From burdened sinners fees extort;
No sacred beast nor sacred birds
  To which the knee is bent with awe,
No rites unclean, nor mumbled words,
  Nor magic arts, I heard or saw.

No more with self-inflicted pains
  The hermit thought to purge his sin;
Nor wild fanatic racked his brains
  For some new mode by which to win
A higher plain of life at last.
  The Brahmin priest no more denied
The rights of those of lower caste:
  Distinctions all were laid aside.

The widow, once the butt of scorn
  And cruel taunts, held as a slave,
Bereft of hope, living forlorn,
  In wistful longings for the grave,

Now cherished with affection true,
  Was made to feel love's genial beam,
Accept the honor justly due,
  And rest in friendship's warm esteem.

Llamas and monks had disappeared,
  And praying wheels had passed away
In Thibet, and the gods once feared
  Had gone to ruin and decay.

The humble Christian temple stood
  Where once the heathen shrine had been,
Where priests and nuns, a lecherous brood,
  Indulged in practices unclean.

I looked for crippled feet, but none
  In flowery China could be found;
The daughter welcomed as the son
  From cruel fetters was unbound;
The female babe, no more despised,
  Was reared with tender love and care,
Her favor sought, her graces prized,
  Of social rights enjoyed her share.

The opium dens had been suppressed,
  Their baneful influence all was dead,
With temperate habits all were blest,
  The sick were nursed, the poor were fed;
To ancient dead no more was paid
  The homage due to God alone;
And former rites had all decayed,
  And idol worship been o'erthrown.

Formosa's tribes, once filled with hate
  And glorying in revengeful deeds,
Thirsting for blood that naught could sate,
  Gloating o'er severed human heads,
Had laid their cruelty aside,
  Their vengeful practices forgot,

No more with blood their fingers dyed,
　But rested peaceful in their lot.

Circassia's daughters bright and fair,
　With golden locks and languid eyes,
Of graceful form and features rare,
　Had ceased to be the Turkman's prize:
And he no longer burned with lust
　And selfish passions base and foul,
But turned with lothing and disgust
　From all that might pollute his soul.

For he had learned to love and know
　Immanuel for sinners slain,
And felt his breast with ardor glow
　Beneath Messiah's gentle reign.
No fancied heaven of carnal bliss
　Where houries witching charms display—
A world more sensual than this—
　Luring his soul in vice astray.

Where once the savage mountain horde
　Eager for war's unholy gain,
Like overwhelming torrents poured
　Down on the fertile vale and plain;
The fear of plunder all was gone,
　In hope the sower cast his seed,
And when the harvest time came on
　Found plenty to supply his need.

In Africa where darkest night
　Of superstition long had lowered,
Till not a star one ray of light
　Did to bewildered feet afford,
Which wandered on in deepest shade,
　Stumbling mid pitfalls in the way,
Not knowing where the pathway led,
　Groping in blindness for the day,

The Son of Righteousness had shed
  His healing beams on either hand;
And golden day its wings had spread
  And smiled serenely o'er the land,
Until the darkness all had flown,
  And heathen rites and bloody feasts
Of human flesh no more were known,
  And beastly practices had ceased.

Where once the wily Jesuit,
  With hardened heart that could not feel,
Sought power by ways that seemed him fit,
  Reckless of others woe or weal;
Shadowed the thrones of earth and planned
  To set up kings and overthrow,
To crush beneath his cunning hands
  And lay all opposition low;

Where bishops held with iron grip
  The reins and steered with wondrous skill,
No opportunity let slip
  To upward climb and higher still,
And live in elegance and pride,
  And revel in ungodly gain
Wrung from the peasant by his side,
  Whose life is spent in toil and pain.

I saw no cowl or mitred head,
  Nor surplice white, nor shaven crown,
Nor idle monk whose daily bread
  Came not by labor of his own,
Nor nuns in lonely cells confined,
  Apart from all that love holds dear,
Where once the captive maiden pined
  In gloom and superstitious fear.

I heard no more the clanking chain
  That bound to earth the toiling slave,

Nor saw the lash with bloody stain,
 Nor heard the driver curse and rave,
Nor heard the weeping mother mourn,
 Wishing the grave their forms might hide,
As loved ones from her breast were torn,
 And hope within her bosom died.

And every custom base and vile,
 On continent from shore to shore,
And on the distant lonely isle,
 Had passed away to come no more;
And no usurper sought to claim
 For self the rights to others due;
The great, the small enjoyed the same;
 No grasping by the favored few.

I looked with wonder and delight
 And thought, indeed, can this be true?—
The scene that met my ravished sight
 Thrilled all my being through and through—
Does this the future represent,
 This tranquil scene that meets my view?
Will man his former course relent
 Till God his pristine state renew?

My guide then from his bosom took
With reverend care God's Holy Book,
And read the promise where 'tis said
The seed shall bruise the serpent's head;
And Jacob's blessing which unseals
The future and to man reveals
In cheerful words of prophecy,
The glorious gathering that shall be
When Shilo shall the scepter hold,
And watch in love o'er Zion's fold.

And David's song, that God shall bring
The heathen subject to the King

That he has set on Zion's hill,
When he his promise shall fulfill,
That Christ shall all the earth possess,
With righteous laws the nations bless;

And the rapt prophet's holy lays
That tell of brighter coming days,
When to the people shall be given
The God-child, prince of earth and heaven,

Whose reign shall widen and increase
On David's throne, nor ever cease;
When man shall bloody strife abhor,
And beat the implements of war
To useful tools and dwell content,
His powers no more to evil bent,
Beneath his fruitful vine and tree,
With all the world in harmony;
When all lands for his law shall wait,
And prince and peasant, small and great,
To him shall bend in homage low,
And learn with joy his will to know.

Of mighty empires overthrown
And crushed and scattered by the stone
Seen in night visions on his bed,
By Babylonia's crowned head,
That to a mountain shall expand
Until its presence fills the land.

And Daniel's vision of the time
When Christ shall reign in every clime,
And all dominions 'neath the sky
Shall serve the Majesty on high.

And words that Micah penned when he
The future glory seemed to see,
When to the mountain of the Lord,
The tribes of man with one accord

Shall say, come let us quickly go
To Zion's hill, that we may know
And learn God's precepts to obey,
And walk in his appointed way;
For from his courts, Jerusalem,
He shall to us the law proclaim;
And the glad news that Babylon's whore
Shall fall and sink to rise no more,
And Satan from his seat be hurled,
And all the nations of the world
To Christ, of love, their tribute bring,
And hail Immanuel lord and king.

My guide then disappeared, and I
  Awoke from slumbering on the green
Beneath a ruby morning sky,
  With naught but verdant leafy screen,
Held by the overhanging tree,
  The distant vault and me between;
From every murmuring thought set free,
  My mind was buoyant and serene.

Address To My Soul.

My soul, what are thy hopes? Do things of earth,
Whose swift decay commences with their birth,
Which vanish like the morning mist away,
Or like the transient cloud of summer day,
Take all thy thoughts? Shall the immortal mind
Be all absorbed with such, or can it find
In these a satisfying portion? Nay;
These are too empty, and too brief their stay.

Who drinks at earthly springs tries but in vain
To quench his thirst; he drinks and thirsts again;
And as the water sparkles to his eye,
He tries again his thirst to satisfy;
Though mocked so oft he fondly lingers still
By the enchanting founts; nor can the ill
That they have brought him clear his dazzled sight;
They charm him still, and Reason takes her flight.

But when the solemn hour of death draws near,
How vain will all the joys of sense appear!
They cannot cheer our passage through the gloom—
The shadows dark which hover o'er the tomb—
Nor shed across our path one glimmering ray
To guide our feet along the lonely way;
Nor will we find them on the other shore;
They'll fade and disappear to rise no more.

As a weary traveler on the desert wild,
Parched 'neath the sun, by phantom scenes beguiled,
Sees in the distance far the shimmering lake,
And hastens on his burning thirst to slake,

But only finds a dreary waste of sand;
So pilgrims, passing through time's barren land,
Fancy they see ahead a refreshing stream
Of earthly bliss, and find it but a dream.

The Prodigal for other joys would roam
Than those that clustered round his native home,
But came to want; so man, from God apart,
Finds famine ever gnawing at his heart,
Till sorely pressed his famished soul would dine
On empty husks, and grovel with the swine;
Pining for happiness the world ne'er gives;
Dead to substantial joy—dead while he lives.

Yet I would not these earthly gifts disdain—
They fill their place—neither would I refrain
From any joy that God would have me taste—
He knows my every want—but I would haste
From all that might ensnare my feet and flee,
Nor turn to look on the forbidden tree,
But look to Him with holy, grateful love,
And fix my longing heart on things above.

Why should we from the living God depart
And set up earthly idols in our heart?
In Him alone is found enduring peace—
Pure streams of joy whose flow shall never cease;
And brighter grows the prospect on before,
Till things of time and sense can charm no more;
Till the enraptured soul would gladly fly
To its divine abode, its native sky.

One makes a god of wealth, and offers praise
And odors sweet, and on the altar lays
His sacrifice; the first fruits of his toil,
The firstlings of his beasts and all the spoil

That he has won, the tenth of all his grain,
And wine and oil, the fat of creatures slain
And blood and other offerings set apart,
He offers with a free and constant heart.

But what is his reward? Is he at rest?
Does harrowing guilt no more disturb his breast?
Is fear all gone? Has Conscience sheathed her sting?
Does Hope brood o'er his soul with balmy wing?
Do strains divine entrance his listening ear?
And to his sight do visions bright appear,
A foretaste rich of brighter joys to be
When time has flown and dawned eternity?

Nay verily; a galling load he bears
Of eager, anxious thoughts and cankering cares,—
The fear of loss oft times disturbs his ease;
He seeks for rest, but rest forever flees,
E'en in the silent watches of the night,
Though wooed on downy couch, sleep takes its flight
And leaves him to the mercy of his fears
And tossings to and fro till dawn appears.

One makes a deity of his own flesh,
Whom he displeases oft yet tries afresh,
With curious art and every strange device,
His god to suit, in ways select and nice;
But more he does the less he seems to please;
Naught can its clamoring appetites appease;
He finds a cumbrous idol on his hands;
The more he gives the more his god demands.

The goddess Pride, twin born with Vanity—
How many willing worshipers has she!
Deep in the heart she sets her dazzling throne
Till she and Vanity and self are one.

Was ever other such strange trinity?
Or can there stranger worship ever be?
The worshiper himself is deified,
And kneels to self as he bows down to Pride.

But is he blest? Does pure substantial joy
Dwell richly in his heart without alloy?
Does Love lay her soft hand upon his heart
And cure its every ill and soothe each smart,
And bathe his brow in waves of heavenly light,
And upward bear his soul in tireless flight?
Does all his being chime with melody?
Restful his breast as tranquil summer sea?

What are the fruits? What does this worship bring?
Longing and discontent and envying,
Malice and jealousy and hate and spite,
And else in which a friend might take delight.
This poison fruit, though bringing woe and pain,
At Pride's command is eaten oft again;
Though often nauseating to the taste
Like drunkard's cup 'tis sought again with haste.

Who worships self, worships a god of clay
Which soon will fall and crumble to decay,
And blast his hopes and disappoint his trust,
And lay his brightest visions in the dust;
Then all his pride will moulder low as he,
And all the glittering traps of vanity;
The naked spirit then when hope has fled
Will mourn in bitter grief her idols dead.

The goddess Fashion, fickle as the wind,
Adored by all the ranks of human kind,
Who follow blindly in her lengthened train,
Holds o'er our race a more extended reign

Than all beside, and sways with magic skill
Her gaudy scepter o'er the human will;
And eager multitudes on bended knee,
Bow down to this fantastic deity.

The simpering belle, the dame with silvered hair,
The sad, the gay, the ugly and the fair,
The robust youth puffed up with self conceit,
The aged sire who moves with cautious feet,
The man of leisure free from anxious care,
And he of toil reduced to humble fare,
The serf, the prince, the king upon his throne,
The pauper, all her cunning witchery own.

She finds her willing subjects on the farm,
And lures its dwellers with some mystic charm;
The poor mechanic grovels 'neath her bond,
The merchant feels the magic of her wand;
The lawyer, banker, preacher, statesman feel
Bound to her service with a band of steel;
She holds the church, the state, the shop, the school,
The great and small, the learned and the fool.

The things that she admires the same do they,
And those that she rejects they cast away;
Nor do they for a reason stop to ask,
But bend with vigor to the endless task
Of doing what tomorrow will undo,
Charmed with the novelty of aught that's new
In modes and manners, furniture and dress,
In styles, and in religion none the less.

Her lips are full of flattery and deceit,
And modesty lies trampled 'neath her feet;
She drives the gentler graces from the breast,
And fills the soul with longing and unrest;

Incites to lust and passion's base desire
That burns up all that's pure like raging fire
That fiercer glows till cold, relentless death
Quenches the vivid flame with icy breath.

How many precious moments go to waste,
How much of toil, to suit her changeful taste!
What wealth is squandered that might feed the poor,
Or carry comfort to the sick man's door!
Enlighten those who sit in darkest night,
And lift them from their sad and hopeless plight,
Or spread in darkened heathen lands afar
The light of Christ, the bright and morning star!

Some pressed with galling burdens hard to bear,
Cumbered with debts and crushed with anxious care,
Tortured like victims on the cruel rack,
Add other burdens to their weary back
To please this fickle dame and lead the van
Of the vast throng that hear and heed her ban,
Till ruin swallows all their earthly store
And leaves them stranded, hopeless, aimless, poor.

What will she give, or how will she repay
For all the time and labor thrown away
In the vain chase to satisfy her whims?
When Death's fell blow the mortal eye bedims,
What will the unclothed spirit then descry
In her, vain empty things to satisfy
The immortal longings of the deathless soul
In the beyond as endless ages roll?

And shall we tamely yield to her demands
And let her rule us with unsparing hands,
Absorb our thoughts and rob us of our gains,
Despoil us quite till nothing worth remains,

To naked stand in that great solemn day,
When all the things of time have passed away,
Before the Judge to learn our dreadful lot
And hear the words, "Depart, I know you not?"

No, let us lay her glittering baubles by,
Prepare for that bright world beyond the sky;
Bathed in the golden light of endless day,
Where all is pure, where peace and love holds sway,
That we with confidence our Lord may meet
And find a gracious welcome at his feet,
To gaze with wonder on his radiant face,
His sacred wounds and form of matchless grace.

On cold Parnassus' steep and rugged height,
Girt round with snow, on throne of dazzling white,
Sits beckoning Fame on icy royalty
Waving his wand to struggling devotee
Who seems to see in fancy's wildering light
Beside the throne his name in letters bright,
Willing to pray, to labor and endure,
His calling and election to insure.

What endless toils to gain an empty name!
The joys that others seek, to him how tame!
What musings long that bid sweet sleep depart,
What hopes deferred, what pantings of the heart,
What restless energy, what strong desire,
That his poor fellow creatures may admire
In time to come his deathless name enrolled
On Fame's bright page in characters of gold!

The joys of love, of sweet domestic bliss,
The glancing eye, the fond endearing kiss,
The witching smile that bathes the glowing face,
The hand's soft pressure and the warm embrace,

Have not the power his eager soul to charm,
Nor the sole purpose of his life disarm,
But all his faculties are made to bend
To the accomplishment of one lone end.

The prattling babe brim full of noisy glee
That climbs and romps upon a parent's knee,
Smoothing his hair with its soft finger tips
And planting kisses with sweet rosy lips,
Or, weary grown, sinking to peaceful rest
With drooping head against his bosom prest,
Has only power to wake a passing thought;
Fame drinks him up; all else is soon forgot.

His soul grows frigid as the northern seas;
Across it floats no genial summer breeze;
'Tis dreary as a waste of Arctic snow,
Where naught that seeks the warmth of love can grow
Where winter reigns with unrelaxing sway,
Where lights boreal shoot their boding ray
That charms the eye, but can no heat impart
To melt the ice that gathers round the heart.

These gods will disappoint us by and by;
Though seeming fair each promise is a lie;
They lure us on with phantoms passing bright,
And shed along our path bewildering light,
But fail to help us in the time of need;
Who leans on them leans on a broken reed;
They have no power to bring the weary rest,
No healing balm to sooth the aching breast.

Even the blessings that attend our lives—
The creature comforts God so freely gives,
Strewn thick along our path on either side,
And empty bubbles floating on life's tide,

And flitting shadows light and void as they
Take up the thoughts and draw the mind away
From things above in yonder blest abode—
The Christians' home—the Paradise of God.

Can we afford to give up heaven for such?
Away so base a thought! heaven means too much—
Pleasures as fadeless as the great white throne,
Abiding still when countless years have flown;
While things below, however bright they seem,
Are only transient as the morning dream;
We hug them to our breast and call them ours;
They droop within our arms like withered flowers.

My mind turns back to childhood's sunny day,
When on my path no gloomy shadows lay;
A mother's blessing rested on my head
And o'er my heart its hallowed influence shed;
The smile upon her face again I see,
In fancy take my place beside her knee;
Again in tones of love I hear her speak,
And feel the warm kiss on my willing cheek.

Her flesh now moulders in its native clay;
Her spirit basks in heaven's effulgent ray,—
How soon they passed, those joys so rich and pure!
Alas! there's nothing earthly can endure;
The summons comes, we stretch our hands in vain;
Death heeds us not, though hearts are rent in twain;
Yet, blessed thought, in yonder blissful clime,
Joys shall endure unmarred by changeful time.

The friends of early youth no more I see;
Asundered far, I know not where they be,
Save some who in their earthly chambers sleep,
And one who lies beneath the briny deep.

Though memory often holds them in review,
Love's broken ties time never can renew.
Oh! shall we meet in fairer worlds again
Where partings bring the heart no bitter pain?

The airy castles that I used to build,
Frail as a breath, with fancied treasures filled,
Have all gone down beneath the rolling years,
Till not a vistage of their form appears;
Built on the sand, not on the solid rock,
How could they stand the raging tempest's shock?
And hopes as brilliant as the rainbow hue
Have vanished like the early morning dew.

The path I pondered never felt my tread;
From it I walked apart as I was led
By hand unseen, yet safely on the way
Mid devious paths that call the feet astray,
And cause to wander from the narrow road
That leads the soul to happiness and God.
I have not run the mazy course alone,
My feet were led by wisdom not my own.

Youth passed away and robust manhood came;
My bosom glowed with Hymen's genial flame;
I sought my mate and brought her to my side
To breast with me the swellings of the tide;
We found our place and built our quiet nest,
And she in me and I in her were blest;
And nestlings came our cup of joy to fill
And make our hearts with social pleasures thrill.

Oh! such are joys that God delights to see;
They fill the soul with heaven's own melody,
And make our pathway sunny as the moon,
But, Oh! they die and pass away so soon;

Death hovers nigh and lays his withering hand
On all that's dear, and breaks each social band,
And tears the loved ones from our fond embrace,
Blasts all our plans and mocks us to our face.

The chosen one that walked the vale with me,
From all the cares and toils of time set free,
On the cold earth laid down her weary head,
To calmly sleep within her narrow bed
And wait the welcome summons from the skies
That wakes the dead and bids the sleeper rise
Arrayed in pure and spotless robes divine,
That shall the splendor of the sun outshine.

One little boy lies mouldering low as she
Beneath the mound upon the grassy lea;
No sounds of earth disturb his slumbers deep;
Asleep in Jesus! Sweet and peaceful sleep
That knows no waking till the Saviour comes
With trumpet sound to rouse the silent tombs
And call the sleepers from their lone retreat,
And all the powers of death and hell defeat.

Borne onward by the ceaseless tide of time
Through childhood, youth, and up to manhood's prime,
Their noisy sports and youthful dreams all o'er,
The loved ones gather round my board no more
As in the days gone by, save now and then;
And some perhaps I'll never see again
Until we stand before Christ's judgment seat
Where the assembled universe shall meet.

Low in the west descends the setting sun;
The shadows lengthen as the night comes on;
I backward look across the fading years,
And scan the groundless hopes and needless fears

That lead me zigzag through the wildering maze
Where shades alternate with bright cheering rays,
And wonder that my feet escaped the snares
So deftly set to take me unawares.

And as my vision clears I plainly see
'Twas God's unerring hand that guided me,
Sometimes o'er barren mountains rough and steep,
Sometimes through troubled waters cold and deep,
Yet oft through smiling meadows bright and green,
By verdant groves and many a fairy scene,
Leading my weary feet along the road,
Imparting strength when sinking 'neath my load.

Oh! had I ever walked as God would lead,
In patience ran the race nor slacked my speed,
Nor turned aside to taste forbidden joys
And waste the precious hours on worthless toys,
The many blots that darken memory's page,
Strewn all along through every varying stage,
Would not have blurred the plainly written lines
Recording there his bountiful designs.

But wayward self oft sought to walk alone
The course that seemed him best, in ways his own,
In hidden paths by him before untrod,
With helmet gone and tender feet unshod,
With girdle loosed, no breastplate, sword, or shield
To meet the foe on life's stern battlefield
And turn him back, and quench the fiery darts
That Satan hurls with all his hellish arts.

God loved me still, his angel hovered near;
His gentle chidings fell upon my ear:
"Why will you walk the downward path of sin?
This is the way of life, come walk therein;

Thy soul is precious, why wilt thou delay
To turn and walk in God's appointed way?"
Till weary grown, with shame and guilt oppressed,
I sought my Lord and found my spirit's rest.

Who drinks the healing waters Jesus gives,
Though dead with thirst, his famished spirit lives;
His soul his native buoyancy regains,
The quickened pulse throbs joyfully in his veins,
The broken bones are healed, the leprous flesh
All disappears, and youth returns afresh;
He runs the race appointed to the saints
And wearies not, he walks and never faints.

He turns away from sin's delusive cup,
No more he drinks its deadly poison up;
The tempting goblet dashes from his lips;
No more in stagnant pool his vessel dips;
Within his soul the healing waters rise,
A pure and sparkling spring that never dries;
Not winter's chilly bands of ice and snow,
Nor summer's drought can stop its genial flow.

Melodious sounds now fill his listening ears—
The chiming melody of distant spheres—
He hears the rustle of angelic wings,
A voice within his breast responsive sings,
And as the music through his being floats,
He lists with rapture to the swelling notes;
Silence no more sits on his loosened tongue,
He joins the heavenly choir with grateful song.

Though long he walked in sad and dismal plight,
Groping his way through gloomy shades of night,
Stumbling o'er rocks, with torn and bleeding feet,
While pelting storms against his bosom beat,

By some delusive ignis-fatuus led,
That shone a moment on his path then fled,
To reappear and disappear again
And leave him wildered on life's dreary plain.

He now beholds the cheering dawn of day,
The night recedes, the shadows flee away;
O'er eastern hills he sees the sun arise
And march in splendor up the glowing skies;
The ghostly phantoms of the past have flown;
His gladdened soul now basks in radiant noon;
The breath of heaven through all his being flows;
With life and ardent love his bosom glows.

And as he looks adown the western slope,
His breast expands, his heart grows big with hope,
He sees beyond the waters dark and cold
The crystal pavement on the streets of gold
By myriad feet of saints and angels trod,
And waters issuing from the throne of God,
With verdant trees of life on either side—
A living stream that flows with gentle tide.

When hope had well-nigh yielded to despair,
Homesick and fainting from his meagre fare,
With want and sorrow pictured on his face
He came to seek a servant's humble place,
The Father knew afar his wayward child,
Though clad in tattered garments dust defiled,
With yearning bosom sought his side in haste,
With welcome kiss his long-lost son embraced.

He roams no more, contented to abide
Where peace and plenty smile on either side,
In goodly land where milk and honey flow,
And choicest grains in rich profusion grow,

And fruits delicious borne on tree and vine,
A land of healing balm and oil and wine,
Of hills and vales and springs and running brooks,
Of pastures green, a land of herds and flocks.

And he exults o'er brighter days to come
When, past the vale, he finds his endless home
In fairer worlds, beyond the bounds of time
Where spring abides, a never-fading clime;
There healthfulness pervades the ambient air,
No waning moons nor burning suns are there;
There pearly gates and many mansions gleam
With the pure light of God and of the Lamb.

Though pain be mixed with every earthly joy
And Satan mar what he may not destroy,
Though persecutions fall upon his head
And foes increase and friends afar have sped,
Though all his works, with patient labor wrought,
And all his cherished plans have come to naught,
Yet on his path a beck'ning light appears
That brightens hopes and scatters all his fears.

He knows that heaven will recompense his pain,
That joys unsullied there forever reign,
There sin and Satan can no more molest
Nor pain disturb, nor sorrow e'er distress;
No weeping there above the fallen dead,
No breaking hearts, no bitter tears are shed,
No passions dark, no sighs, no harrowing fears,
But peace and joy through all the rolling years.

.. Shorter Poems ..

The Golden Hour.

The sun was by the clouds concealed,
  The air was chill from recent shower,
A mist hung over wood and field,
  And yet it was a sunny hour.

The leaves were dripping wet with rain,
  And humbly bowed was each sweet flower,
While bent to earth were grass and grain,
  But still it was a radiant hour:

For 'neath the cottage roof there shone
  A light of wondrous warmth and power,
That melted kindred hearts in one,
  And glowed in every passing hour.

It was the calm pure light of love
  That makes of earth an Eden's bower,
Joined with that radiance from above
  That gilds the Christian's darkest hour.

The wife and mother's gentle grace,
  The children playing on the floor,
The tender kiss, the fond embrace—
  Oh! these can make a golden hour.

When shadows to your spirit come,
  And clouds and tempest darkly lower
Cherish the light of heaven and home;
  T'will make of time a sunny hour.

The Brevity of Earthly Good.

They come and go, the fleeting years,
  With silent step they glide away
And hasten on, nor heed our tear,
  Nor for our joys one moment stay.

They come and go, our hopes and fears,
   Like flitting clouds of summer day—
A shadow on our path appears,
   Succeeded by a golden ray.

They come and go, these earthly joys,
   Like bubbles on the rippling stream:
We find them only transient toys;
   Their light is but a passing gleam.

How soon they fade, these mortal forms—
   Death's cruel hand brooks no delay—
Till, crushed beneath time's wintry storms,
   They sink to darkness and decay!

But as the day succeeds the night,
   So an eternal morn shall rise
And scatter far its healing light,
   And gild with glory all the skies.

Then let them pass, these earthly things;
   We would not wish their flight to cease,
But let them haste on rapid wings,
   Till dawns that welcomed day of peace.

No more the years shall come and go,
   Nor torturing fears our souls dismay;
Joy like a river then shall flow,
   And Love o'er all her scepter sway.

The Coming Day.

All hail the day when God shall turn
   Earth to its pristine state again,
When evil passions cease to burn,
   And love shall in man's nature reign.

This earth has long been drunk with blood,
　Has reeled, bewildered, to and fro;
Vile sin has swept it like a flood
　Whose muddy waters ceaseless flow.

But by and by a day shall dawn
　When war and strife shall be no more;
Then man shall righteousness put on,
　His Maker honor and adore.

Then all the race shall brothers be,
　And love shall glow in every breast;
From dark and selfish passions free,
　Earth shall rejoice and man be blest.

The Beauties of Nature.

How beautiful the works of God!
　How lovely! how divine!
O'er all this bright, green earth abroad,
　Unnumbered beauties shine.

How lovely verdant vale and hill,
　And tangled woodland wild,
And shady nook, and dancing rill
　With music soft and mild!

What beauty in the stream that speeds
　Mid forest wilds and bowers,
O'er pebbly beds, through verdant meads
　Decked o'er with smiling flowers!

And how entrancing is the night
　When on the landscape wide,
Luna looks down and sheds her light
　O'er field and dancing tide!

And e'en the mad, wild winds that seem
  Of their own fury proud,
And lurid lightenings as they gleam
  From out their murky cloud.

And muttering thunders as they roar,
  And waves that madly roll
And dash against the rocky shore,
  Charm and delight the soul.

Toil.

Ne'er despise an honest calling;
  If you're faithful, though 'tis low,
Brightest blessings ceaseless falling,
  God shall on your head bestow.

Why should man become elated,
  Scorning humble, honest toil?
God has labored, has created;
  Fitting labor is not moil.

Toil is God-like, 'tis exalting,
  Lifting man toward Deity;
Nature toileth, never halting,
  Onward to eternity.

Worlds are rolling, suns are shining,
  Comets wheeling to and fro,
Days are dawning and declining,
  Changing seasons come and go.

Toil will give us, never ceasing,
  Happy thoughts forever bright,
Harmless joys with age increasing,
  Make our hearts and footsteps light.

Twilight Fancies.

The golden sun has sunk to rest
Behind the woodland of the west,
And, casting back a rosy smile,
Left earth to silent night awhile.

The day with all its hopes and fears,
Its joy and gloom, its smiles and tears,
Its painful toils and revels gay,
Has passed, forever passed away.

And many a flower has drooped its head,
No more its sweet perfume to shed;
Yea, human flowers of loveliest bloom
Have sunk into the silent tomb.

And there they'll calmly, sweetly sleep,
And friends will gather there to weep,
And learn that they must also die
And in the cold earth mouldering lie.

And virtue, too, that priceless flower,
Has faded, withered in an hour;
Seared by temptation's blighting frost,
In many a heart its charms are lost.

And where it grew there weeds will start,
And thorns shall rise to pierce that heart,
And all its verdure fade away,
And what was lovely soon decay.

O wandering soul! return, return,
And bid thy passions cease to burn,
And quench the wild, consuming fire,
Pluck in its bud each vile desire.

To Hope.

O bright-winged Hope! be thou my stay
  When waves of trouble o'er me roll;
Lift up thy lamp to cheer my way,
  Be thou the anchor of my soul.

Help me the tide of life to brave,
  Along the way my steps attend,
And when my journey nears the grave,
  Be thou my unassuming friend.

If thou art with me thou canst cheer
  And turn my darkest night to day;
Before thy radiant form pale Fear
  Hasteth in silent mood away.

Say, why shouldest thou desert thy throne
  And yield it up to wan Despair,
When life with blessings has o'erflown,
  While I its richest gifts may share?

For me the earth with plenty teems
  To fill my every pure desire;
For me the sun with golden beams
  Emits its recreating fire.

For me the whispering winds go by,
  The brooklets murmur soft and low;
The storm-clouds sweep across the sky,
  The mighty waters ebb and flow,

The moon looks down from yonder blue,
  The stars dispense their twinkling light;
Mild Autumn glows with varied hue,
  And Winter spreads his carpet white;

Sweet Spring returns with balmy air,
  Her richest bounty, Summer yields,
Scatters her gifts with lavish care
  O'er hills and valleys, woods and fields.

But more, for me the Savior died,
  And paid my ransom with his blood;
And soon he'll call me to his side,
  Close to the dazzling throne of God.

Were half the blessings I enjoy,
  Were half my comforts told to thee;
Pale sickening Fear it would destroy,
  And thou would'st reign triumphantly.

The Sentinel's Vision.

The sentinel paced by the river's lone side,
  While the stars were lit up in the sky's blue expanse;
But he saw not the gleam of their light on the tide,
  For his spirit was rapt with the sweets of a trance.

His soul was aglow as he thought of his home,
  Of the joy and the peace that awaited him there,
When, his services ended, the glad hour would come
  When he with the loved ones its pleasures would share.

He saw in his fancy the smile on her face
  Whose heart beat responsive in love to his own,
And folded her form in a tender embrace,
  And whispered a blessing in love's gentle tone.

And he pictured his babes, with their bright sparkling eyes,
  Their round rosy cheeks and their soft flaxen hair,
As they stood by his side or climbed on his knees,
  Each anxious his love and attention to share.

He turned, and his dream like a spirit took wing,
  But it left a bright radiance of hope in his breast,
That time of his vision the real would bring,
  When he with the charms of sweet home would be blest.

Let's Be Merry.

Let's be merry, let's be merry;
    Though old Winter's icy frown
Makes the world look cold and dreary,
    Let mild social mirth go round.

What's the use of being moody?
    Winter will not frown the less;
'Twill not warm or clothe the body,
    Nor its clamoring wants suppress.

Plenty o'er the land is smiling;
    Toil has reaped a rich reward;
Now let love, our hearts beguiling,
    Hush each fretful clamorous word.

If we sorrow, let us sorrow
    That temptation stalks abroad,
Bringing shadows for the morrow
    To sad souls away from God.

You who harbor fancied evils,
    Would you feel a cheering ray?
Go where in cold, cheerless hovels
    Want keeps gnawing night and day.

Carry thither food and clothing;
    Let your gifts be large and free;
Utter something tender, soothing,
    And the demons all will flee.

Let's be merry, let's be sorry;
    Let's be merry as we should:
Let us sorrow that we borrow
    Care instead of doing good.

My Baby.

Cold blows the wind and to the fire
    My chair is drawn, and on my knee
My baby sits and to its sire
    Is playing, cooing merrily.

Thou little one, the wealth of earth
    I would not take and part with thee:
Thy merry infant voice is worth
    More than a mine of gold to me.

Thy little fingers as they touch
    My cheek a thrill of pleasure give;
And thy sweet look shall teach me much
    In future life to better live.

Ne'er may an evil word depart
    My lips to marr thy growing mind—
The plant that's injured in the start
    A vigorous growth can never find.

But I will watch with tender care
    Those faculties that God has given,
To keep thy feet from every snare
    And lead thee in the way to heaven.

The Horrors Of War.

Hark! hear you not the dying groan,
    The frenzied shriek, the battle's roar?
See not brave heroes, overthrown,
    Lie weltering in their crimson gore?

The cannons boom with frightful jar;
    On, on the frantic soldiers speed:
Their war shouts rend the startled air;
    The dead nor dying can they heed.

Oh mournful sight! o'er all the plain
    The fallen, mangled warriors lie;
Some dead, some writhing in their pain
    With gaping wound and glaring eye.

There lies a man crushed 'neath the steed
    That bore him midst the battle's roar;
From noisy strife and tumult freed,
    He'll hear the bugle's call no more.

Here lies a clown and here a sage,
    And here a man whose locks are white:
Not fear of death, nor hoary age,
    Could keep them from the bloody fight.

Yonder a youth of goodly form,
    Lies stark in silent death's repose;
No more the rattling drum's alarm
    Will call him forth to meet his foes.

Though strong of limb and brave of soul,
    He could not shun the hand of death:
War breathes alike o'er young and old,
    Ill-formed and fair his withering breath;

Sweeps with destruction o'er the land,
    Cuts down the noble and the brave,
Spreads sorrows wide on either hand,
    Heaps hundreds in one crimson grave.

Warm Hearts.

The window-panes are frosted white,
    And it is freezing very fast;
But yet our hearts are warm and light,
    And merrily the time goes past.

What makes our hearts thus light and warm?
    'Tis love that burns with heavenly glow.
What care we for the out-door storm
    When o'er our souls warm zephyrs blow?

But, ah! suppose a storm should rise
    Within and it should wildly blow;
However balmy were the skies,
    Our hearts would soon be filled with snow.

The Christian Home.

How bright and happy is that home
    Where love and harmony abide!
This earth an Eden shall become
    When strife and selfishness subside.

Around that home where love holds sway
    There floats an atmosphere serene,
That makes pale, cankering fear decay,
    And lightens up the distant scene;

Bids Hope lift up her banner high,
    And Courage onward press amain;
Dries up the tear and stills the sigh,
    Heals every wound, soothes every pain.

Let proud Ambition seek for bliss
    Amid the sterile peaks of fame;
They'll greet him with an icy kiss,
    And yield him but an empty name.

Let misers walk amid their store
    And gaze upon the glittering heap,
And count their treasures o'er and o'er
    While weary nature lies asleep.

Let epicures in cellars shy
    Corrupt the crimson stream of life,
And sensualists of deeper dye
    Forget the bonds of man and wife.

Let wanderers seek from pole to pole,
    Or to the distant island roam;
There's naught of earth that fills the soul
    Like the unrivaled charms of home.

O home! sweet home! the Christian's home,
    Where man and wife are joined in love,
And children in the bud and bloom,
    All in harmonious union move!

Man Compared To a Meteor.

The day had gone, the cool, refreshing night
    Had flung its shadows o'er the slumbering world,
The stars looked down with beams as bright and pure
    As when the map of nature first unfurled.

And as I gazed upon yon spangled dome,
    I saw from out the misty depths of space
A meteor shoot across the midnight gloom
    And disappear, nor leave a single trace.

How like is man! he rises from the dust
    And shines awhile with scintillating flame,
Then, helpless, falls before death's cruel thrust,
    To moulder in the earth from whence he came.

Though he, perhaps, in characters of blood
    Has stamped his title on the page of fame,
And poured out woe and anguish like a flood,
    Yet, meteor-like, he disappears the same.

Perhaps in costly lore he may excel,
   And shed around a pure enlightening glow,
And mists and darkness from his sphere expel;
   Death scruples not to crush him at a blow.

May-be in moral worth his name stands high,
   His heart may every social grace possess,
In virtue clad as radiant as the sky;
   Yet the cold clod down on his form shall press.

Today he rises, sheds a transient ray,
   Tomorrow finds him sleeping in the tomb:
A worm, a creature of a fleeting day,
   He disappears and others fill his room.

The Drunkard's Wife.

Sadly the wife of the drunkard recalls
   Beautiful scenes of her childhood's bright home;
Dark on her pathway the shadow now falls,
   Shrouding her future in fathomless gloom.

Sweet was the vision that glittered like gold,
   When in the dawning of womanhood's day,
She felt in her being new longings unfold,
   Promising pleasures that should not decay.

When on the altar of Hymen was laid
   Freely the wealth of her love, warm and pure,
Costly indeed was the price that she paid
   For a dream only, that did not endure.

Brief was the bliss that enraptured her soul;
   Long has she wandered apart from the light:
Lo, the deep curse of the inebriate's bowl
   Fell on her life, a dark, withering blight

Mem'ry now taunts her with joys that are dead,
　　Specters peer out from the mist on before;
Hope from her sorrowing bosom has fled;
　　Stranded her bark on despair's sullen shore.

To York River.

River, sweet river, how tranquil thy breast,
　　Glancing the sunlight untouched by the storm!
Calm as the face of an infant at rest,
　　With arms of a mother entwined round its form.

Yet thou can'st rage and thy waters can splash
　　As tempests sweep o'er thee in maddening roar,
And thy wild waves in fury and anger can dash
　　Like demons of passion in foam on the shore.

Then the white gull with his tapering wing,
　　Wheeling and screaming above thee on high,
Longing for food that the tempest might bring,
　　Searches thy bosom with ravenous eye.

Vessels lie moored on thy bosom at rest,
　　Or spread their white sails and glide softly away,
Or shoot like an arrow and dash down the crest
　　Of the billow that dances and scatters its spray.

Yonder spread out lies the broad sandy plain
　　Where Washington captured our liberty's foe,
Oh! that was a stunning blow, never again
　　The power that they once enjoyed monarchs shall know.

There, too, Oppression turned back in dismay,
　　When McClellan had marshaled his host for the fight,
As heroes undaunted rushed into the fray,
　　And heroes as fearless were scattered in flight.

Peace now is smiling upon thy green shore,
    Ne'er may the battle cry ring here again;
The chain of the bondman shall clank here no more,
    But Liberty o'er thy fair borders shall reign.

River, sweet river, how tranquil thy rest!
    Mirror of heaven, thy smooth, glassy form:
May thy tranquility reign in my breast,
    Hushing forever dark passion's wild storm.

The Calm That Jesus Brings.

The waves were high on Galilee,
    And onward rushed with angry roar,
As wild winds swept across the sea,
    And dashed them on the rugged shore:
Strong men were struggling at the oar
    To force their passage o'er the deep;
In vain they sought the land before,
    While Jesus lay in quiet sleep.

They called him from his place of rest,
    In terror of a watery grave;
The tempest lulled at his behest;
    The dashing waters ceased to rave,
But kissed the boat with gentle lave,
    And rippled softly to the land.
Along the beach the dimpled wave
    Expired in murmurs on the sand.

My soul by sin and sorrow prest,
    Borne on the waves with terrors strown,
Sought all in vain a place of rest,
    And rose and sank with bitter groan:
I struggled, weary and alone,
    Against the onward-rushing tide,
Till all the joy of life had flown,
    And every hope within me died.

I turned to him with longing eyes,
　　Who stilled the raging of the sea,
And bade its billows cease to rise,
　　And stretched my hands imploringly;
With words of cheer He came to me
　　And hushed the waters all to rest;
And bade my guilt and anguish flee.
　　Aud calmed the tumult in my breast.

To Lake Erie.

O Erie! thou art loved by me;
　　I love to wander by thy side
And sit me down and gaze on thee,
　　Or swiftly o'er thy bosom glide.

I love to view thee when asleep,
　　When not a wave disturbs thy breast,
When all the billows of thy deep
　　Are hushed in silence and in rest.

Oft have I stood upon the shore,
　　When angry winds disturbed thy form,
And listened to the mingled roar
　　As thou combatedst with the storm.

Oft have I sat upon the green
　　Beneath the overhanging tree,
And viewed the ever-changing scene,
　　And listened to thy melody.

Then would my ravished soul rejoice,
　　My cup of joy would overflow,
And I in praise would lift my voice
　　To Him who bids thee come and go.

The Rum Devil.

Remorseless demon, fiend of hell,
 Light fades before his boding frown;
His shadow dark, naught can dispell,
 While every star of hope goes down.

He hovers near with baneful breath
 O'er infant on its mother's knee,
Plants in its veins the seeds of death,
 Laughs at the harvest that shall be;

Obscures the path that leads to joy,
 Sought by the young adventurer's feet;
Well skilled his victim to decoy
 In mazy paths beyond retreat.

He comes in garb of innocence,
 With smile as sweet as flowery May,
And voice as soft with fair pretense
 As insect's note of summer day.

Till round his victims he has thrown
 His bands, which strengthen and increase;
Then mocks to hear their bitter groan,
 And see their struggles for release.

He bids the wife sit brooding, lone,
 O'er days of anguish yet to come,
O'er social joys forever flown,
 And faded hopes and ruined home.

I hear afar the drunken brawl
 Sound out upon the midnight air;
On pavement see the inebriate fall,
 And hear sad wailings of despair.

I hear the children cry for bread,
   And see the pinched and pallid face
And shrunken limbs in tatters clad,
   While wintry winds each other chase.

How many a youth of virtue shorn,
   Caught in the snare this fiend has laid,
Has caused a mother's heart to mourn,
   And bowed in grief a father's head.

Behold the maid that once was fair
   And radiant as the morning sky;
With social instincts rich and rare,
   Which sparkled in her beaming eye.

The teardrops from their fountain spring,
   Alas, the ruin that I see!
Forgetfulness, thy mantle bring,
   And cover all, sweet charity.

I see the drunkard near his end
   When flickers life's expiring flame,
And see him shudder to descend
   Down to the depths of endless shame.

Unmask the demon's ugly form;
   Tear off the garb he loves to wear;
Rain on his head the battle storm
   And drive him from the world afar.

O Jesus! Saviour! Thou alone
   Canst lead to certain victory
Oh! may thy saving strength be shown;
   Thy stately steppings let us see.

Youthful Longings.

Down the vale of life I wander,
   Ever wondering with delight;

Brightest beauties here and yonder
　　Greet and charm my ravished sight;
And my heart is overflowing,
　　Gushing with unnumbered joys,
Brighter, purer, fresher growing—
　　Happiness that never cloys.

Still my soul is ever yearning
　　For a bliss it never knew,
In the future half discerning
　　Social joys of brightest hue,
When adown life's river gliding
　　One shall lay her hand in mine,
Each in other's love confiding
　　All our hopes shall intertwine.

That when hands and feet grow weary
　　With the toiling of the way,
And the path seems dim and dreary,
　　Love may shed its cheering ray;
When as kneel I in devotion,
　　One shall bow beside me there,
And to God with warm emotion
　　Pour with me her soul in prayer.

To A Sister.

The rich may roll in shining wealth,
Bid fashion crush the rose of health,
And revel till in rapid stealth
　　Death thins their ranks;
But happier far thy bosom swelleth
　　'Mid childish pranks.

The flaxen heads that round thee move
Beneath thy ever watchful love
Anchor thy soul, it cannot rove
    Forbidden seas,
But floats in zephyrs far above
    Lust's fatal breeze.

The household cares, the merry ring
Of childish voices, are the spring
Of brighter joys than wealth can bring,
    Or passion knows;
For these oft o'er life's pathway fling
    A cloud of woes.

Idle Dick's Past And Present.

He idly sat and puffed and spat
    Through the sunny summer day;
Though he felt indeed, his pressing need,
    As the swift hours sped away.

The blue smoke curled while the busy world
    Was driving the wheels of trade:
Of the sun and rain and rip'ning grain,
    He seemed to be afraid.

The weeds grew rank and his corn grew lank,
    And the pigs played "hide-and-seek"
In the garden ground and house around,
    While his energy grew weak.

He whined and scowled and snarled and growled
    As he talked of life's hard race,
Of pinching want and hunger gaunt,
    Which stared him in the face.

In the winter days, when the sun's slant rays
    Bring little warmth to earth,
With purple nose and unclad toes,
    His little ones seek the hearth.

And his wife sits down in her faded gown
    On the holy day of rest,
And longs to meet in communion sweet
    With those whom God has blest.

And still he sits and puffs and spits,
    And bows his neck to the yoke,
A slave to a taste bringing want and waste,
    And filth and clouds of smoke.

God's Ways Unsearchable.

Short-sighted man, thy mortal eye,
    Dim, blurred with sin, can never pierce
The veil and solve the mystery
    Why God pours out his vengeance fierce.

But so it is; the maniac's groan,
    The hardened sinner's parting breath,
The dying infidel's last moan,
    Proclaim the burnings of his wrath.

His glorious Word, to mortals given
    To guide them in life's mazy way,
Brings this stern sentence down from heaven:
    "Vengeance is mine; I will repay."

Yet mercy is His chief delight;
    He longs to see the wanderer turn
From error's dark, bewildering night,
    Where sins allure and passions burn.

Then every hostile weapon break;
    Repent and cast away thy pride;
Revolt no more, but come and take
    His Word and Spirit for thy guide.

Spring.

Oh the delights of smiling spring!
    The balmy breath that fans my cheek,
The merry birds that blithely sing,
And through the air their courses wing,
    Some northern nesting place to seek.

The opening flowers that deck the glade,
    Unfolding many colors gay,
Courting the sun or leafy shade,
The grass that shoots its tender blade,
    Bright insects at the close of day.

How lovely are the meadows green!
    How sweet the blossoms on the tree!
How bright the little flowers that screen
Themselves the spears of grass between,
    Peeping so slyly out at me!

The shrubs that stand beside the door
    Load the fresh air with rich perfume,
The cherry blossom's honey store
The bees are culling o'er and o'er,
    The apple shows its fragrant bloom.

How good by murmuring streams to steal
    And sit me down upon the sod,
And spring's enlivening influence feel,
Then by some shady tree to kneel
    And pour my longings out to God;

And worship that Almighty power
    That bids the seasons go their round,
Marks out the sunshine and the shower,
Bids summer smile and winter lower;
    That rules the universe profound.

The Stranger's Baby.

Upon the river's bank there stood
A cottage close beside the wood,
Where vines and shrubs did intertwine,
Not distant from our picket line.

With weary steps I entered there,
The good man bade me take a chair;
I sat me down awhile to chat
Of war and peace, and this and that.

A baby sat upon the floor
And gazed out through the open door,
And as I viewed its little form
I felt my love come gushing, warm.

It quickly brought before my mind
The little ones I left behind,
Who of a father's care deprived,
Alone with mother longing lived.

I took the prattler on my knee
And kissed its sweet lips tenderly;
And as its head my bosom pressed
The pulse leaped joyfully in my breast.

If I Drink, What Then?

If I drink, what good to me
Does it offer? Shall I be
Richer than I was before?
No; but pressed still more and more
For the comforts that I need,
Scanty now enough, indeed.
Hard it is to make my way;
Hard my honest debts to pay.

To the world I justly owe
All the good that I can do:
But with money spent for drink,
Always verging on the brink
Of oppressive want, how can
One deport him like a man?
Fill the place that God designed,
Doing good to human-kind?

Will it more of health impart?
Vigor to the brain and heart?
No; it is a fearful strain
On the heart and clouds the brain;
To the body brings disease,
Pains that rob of joy and ease;
Makes of every power a slave;
Hurries onward to the grave,
Till the light goes out in gloom
Opening into darkest doom.

Will it make our social joys
Brighter? No; it oft destroys
Affection's tie: that silken cord
Once rent, no more our hearts are moored

In sheltered port, but wildly rove
Tossed by the waves; no quiet cove
In which the soul can rest secure,
Bathed in love-light, warm and pure.

Will it give the intellect
Power of vision to detect
What is wrong from what is right?
Does it shed one ray of light
On the path that we should go,
Guiding safely onward? No;
Only gloomy darkness lowers,
Clouding all the mental powers,
Till we grope to find the way,
Lost and wildered, far astray.

Will it bring the soul that rest
Which it longs for? calm the breast?
Bidding all its tumults cease,
Ever giving joy and peace?
No; it makes the future dark,
Present life a burden stark.
All the longings of the soul
Quenched in the accursed bowl,
Naught is left but to descend
Deeper, deeper, to the end.

Reply to a Young Friend.

Yours of the sixth came safe to hand,
And as along the lines I ran,
I saw my friend upgazing stand
        At science's base,
Its rugged side bound to ascend,
        Its summit trace.

What dost thou see on yonder height
That fills thy soul with such delight?
Canst thou discern some diamond bright
    Of truth divine,
That shall o'er earth, dark, lost in night,
    Triumphant shine?

Or dost espy the glittering gold
Of honor, precious to thy soul,
Hoping around thy form to fold
    Bright robes of fame,
And see on some high peak enrolled
    Thy deathless name?

Or dost thy soul for knowledge thirst
And bands of ignorance long to burst?
Was grateful to thy taste the first
    Pure crystal draught?
And hast thou with affection nursed
    The glowing thought?

Whether to bless the human race,
Or honor's shining bubble chase,
Or knowledge with her sunny face
    Demands thy time,
Hold radiant truth with firm embrace,
    Then upward climb.

Throw prejudice to snarling dogs,
Nor check your speed with sensual clogs,
And from the mire of party bogs
    Your garments free;
And rise above the blinding fogs
    Of sophistry.

To A Niece.

You told me dear Niece, that you never would marry;
    But a change has come over your once cherished dreams;

But I hope you may never have cause to be sorry;
   And your life may it glow with prosperity's beams.

And over your days may the moments go gliding,
   And virtue her snowy flowers wreathe on your brow;
And down in your bosom, forever abiding,
   May wells of affection unceasingly flow.

And when to the western horizon descending,
   The last sun of life is hastening apace,
May no gloomy shadows, your memory offending,
   Leave on your changed features, of sorrow, a trace.

O, trust to the One that is willing and able
   To hold thee when Satan would lead thee astray:
Thy strength is but weakness, thy courage unstable;
   The snares of the tempter lie thick on the way.

The Harvest Day.

The quiet shades of night have fled,
   And now at dawning of the day
The farmer rises from his bed
   And to the harvest field away:
With cradle o'er his shoulder swung
   He listens to the morning lay
By many a merry warbler sung,
   High perched upon the slender spray.

Anon he gains the harvest field,
   Swiftly his cradle cleaves the grain;
And now he stops to whet his steel,
   Then plies again with might and main;
And as he views the bending ears,
   He reckons to himself the gain;
'Twill balance all his cares and fears,
   And recompense his toil and pain.

And hope is beaming from his face,
    No cankering cares disturb his mind;
His work is suited to his taste,
    For thus his feelings are inclined:
To live by toil contented he;
    His cheeks would deeply blush to grind
The face of struggling Poverty,
    Or on his shoulders burdens bind.

His fellow-laborers, side by side,
    Follow his footsteps hand in hand,
And now the rustling swaths divide,
    Then deftly draw and tuck the band:
Thus on they labor round and round—
    Perhaps to rest a moment stand,
While mirth and cheerful words abound,
    And pleasing thoughts their souls expand.

Give me the rich, unsullied joys
    That rise up in the harvest hour;
Far brighter than the gilded toys
    Procured by honor, wealth and power:
For these no lasting pleasures bring;
    How vain they seem when sorrow lower;
True joys from higher sources spring;
    The sweets of sense grow stale and sour.

Lullaby.

Hush my sweet baby, the night shadows creep
Over your pillow, go softly to sleep;
Now in your innocence, sleep while you may;
Rude your awaking in life's coming day.

Pilgrim and stranger, yon blissful abode
Beckons you onward in time's mazy road;
Jesus protect you and point you the way,
Guide you from dawn to the close of life's day.

Oft on the wearisome journey you'll find
Anguish of body and sorrow of mind,
Phantoms to lure you from virtue aside,
Bridges to cross o'er the dark surging tide,

Foes to encounter and dangers to pass,
Terrors to startle like snakes in the grass.
Could we but lift the thick curtain and see,
Dumb might our lips with astonishment be.

The Pleasant Autumn Day.

All hail the pleasant autumn day
    That sheds its influence o'er our hearts;
Whose gentle, unoppressive ray
    To each a cheerful tone imparts.

How can we harbor one vile thought
    On such a golden day as this?
Let all unkindness be forgot,
    And let it be a day of peace.

Oh! may its softening influence steal
    Unhindered through our every soul,
And raise our spirits till we feel
    Some wave of heaven across them roll.

It comes at morn with rosy gleam,
    And sweetly smiles when Sol is high;
At evening with mild-tinted beam
    In glory paints the western sky.

The Pleasant Winter Day.

Oh! this has been a golden day,
    Breathing a spirit mild of June:
Methinks some breath from heaven did stray
    To keep our hearts in holy tune.

When Winter howls in fitful storms,
　　Or moans through all the dreary night,
Anxiety our mind alarms,
　　Our thoughts are earthward in their flight

But when the wind is hushed to rest,
　　Or whispers softly from the south,
Joyful emotions swell the breast,
　　And gentle accents fill the mouth.

Then may we open wide our heart
　　And let its genial influence in,
That we to others may impart
　　What this bright day to us has been.

Oh! this has been a golden day,
　　Shedding a halo ronnd each scene;
May we, like its last parting ray,
　　Go out in glory, bright. serene.

The Sailor's Daughter.

A woman's voice had not been heard
　　Since we encamped beside the river;
And there was longing for some word
　　In tones that man ean utter never.

Our eyes of late had been debarred
　　From sight of female grace and beauty;
And weary grown of standing guard
　　In camp and doing picket duty,

We longed for some domestic scene—
　　By some esteemed too tame and common—
For sweet as other joys have been,
　　Still sweeter far the love of woman.

The memory of a mother's smile,
  Her gentle ways and tender greeting,
A sister's love, so free from guile,
  In childhood's hour so bright and fleeting.

The speaking eyes of maiden fair—
  Companion now as well as lover—
And little daught' with flaxen hair,
  Revolved within, over and over.

A vessel on the gleaming tide,
  By anchor held, was calmly riding,
When presently from starboard side
  An open boat came swiftly gliding.

When, lo! in gladness and surprise
  We saw a little form in dresses,
Of slender make and laughing eyes
  And rosy cheeks and silken tresses.

She wore a gown of turkey red,
  But it was not in dress to make her:
A shaker bonnet graced her head:
  Rather her face did grace the shaker.

She was a child, merely a child;
  Her age perhaps might be eleven;
And as she looked around and smiled,
  The brooding from our breast was driven.

To not be glad at such a sight
  Would mark us something less than human;
And we rejoiced with pure delight
  For the rich gift of God—a woman.

Pleasant Scenes Of Childhood.

My birth was by the merry waves
  That dance along Lake Erie's shore,

Kissing the beach with gentle lave,
　　Or raging mid the tempest's roar.
Their murmuring lulled my infant ear,
　　And bound my childhood with their spell,
In youth those notes were ever dear,
　　In manhood's prime I loved them well.

The glassy waters bright and smoothe,
　　Glancing the sun's warm summer ray,
Did oft my childish spirit soothe
　　And drive each stormy thought away.
Those crystal waters still are sweet
　　As when in childhood's dreamy hour
I gazed upon the glittering sheet
　　And felt its strange mysterious power.

The long broad billows heaving high,
　　The wild commotion of the waves,
The angry, cloud-becurtained sky,
　　The noisy wind that wildly raves,
Wake in my breast the same strange chord
　　That trembled in life's opening day,
As seated on the grassy sward
　　I saw and heard thy waters play.

The setting sun's departing ray,
　　Painting the waves with rosy light,
The stretch of waters far away
　　Just on the distant verge of sight;
The low soft murmur of the tide—
　　How does my heart with rapture thrill!
O Eric! fondly by thy side
　　I've lingered oft; I love thee still.

Centennial Musings.

Time flies on rapid wing, it will not stay.
Life is a transient thing that hastes away:

But yesterday the light first met our eye;
Tomorrow comes the night; how soon we die!

But who would spurn this life that God has given,
Thought filled with toil and strife and tempest riven?
A kingdom and a crown lie just before,
Wealth, friendship, and renown on yonder shore.

It is a joy to live, 'twere bliss to die
And feel eternity's bright dawn draw nigh,
But could life naught bestow beyond the grave,
If this short life below is all we have.

If funeral pomp and pall shall be the end,
If to the tomb our all shall then descend,   ·
'Twere better not to be than thus go down;
'Twere better far that we life had not known.

There is a life on high that knows no end;
No clouds obscure yon sky or storms descend:
There pleasure ever dwells without alloy;
There every bosom swells with holy joy.

How can we be content with what's below,
On earthly pleasures bent, that come and go?
The bubbles we pursue, how fair they seem!
Though charming to the view they're but a dream.
Oh! let us fix our home in yon bright sphere
Where sorrows never come, nor pain, nor fear.

Be Kind To The Living.

When the heart has ceased its beating,
    And expired the last faint breath;
When no more we hear the greeting
    Of the lips grown stiff in death:

When the cold thin hands are folded
    Softly on the silent breast;
And the form so deftly moulded
    Sinks into its final rest;

When no more the love-light glances
    In the glassy sightless eye;
And no more the tongue entrances,
    But has said its last goodby.

When the mouldering dust lies sleeping,
    Free from sorrow and distress
Vain were all our feint at weeping
    If in life we failed to bless.

May our minds be ever careful
    All of harshness to restrain,
Ever watching, ever prayerful,
    Lest we give the loved ones pain.

Let our acts and words be tender—
    Balm to heal each bleeding wound,
Looking lest our actions hinder
    Those with whom our lot is bound.

While their presence with us tarries
    Let us feel their pains and woes,
Manifest the love that carries
    Warmth and sunshine where it goes.

May the Savior's love be glowing,
    Burning in our every breast,
To the outside world o'erflowing,
    Bringing happiness and rest.

Seek Not Happiness Below.

Seek not earthly fame and pleasure.
    These are transient as the day:

Lay not up on earth your treasure;
    All of earth will soon decay.

If you find your life, you lose it
    If you seek in things below;
Earth will mock you if you choose it,
    Blind and work your overthrow.

If you lose your life, you find it
    If'tis lost for Jesus' sake:
Fear not, God has thus designed it;
    Life glows at the burning stake.

Fix your heart and hope in heaven
    Where are pleasures that abide;
Struggle onward till the even;
    There is rest beyond the tide.

The Fate of Little Dot.

Little Dot with naked toes,
Tangled hair and tattered clothes,
In a tumble shanty dwelt,
Oft the pangs of hunger felt;
Shivered neath the blankets old,
Through the winter nights so cold.
Sad the life of little Dot;
Father was a drunken sot.

Mother weary, sick and sad—
Few the comforts that she had—
Pining for her childhood's home,
Mind oppressed with fear and gloom;
Brooding o'er her foolish choice,
When against fair reason's voice,
Dazzled by love's blinding ray,
Her young life she threw away

On a youth, beneath whose feet
Hope in ruin sank complete.
She, though of a spirit mild,
Could not cheer her lonely child,
Longing for a mother's care,
In a father's love to share.
Mother, duty heeding not,
Father, poor, degraded sot.

Often in the dead of night
Did she tremble with affright
As the father burst the door,
Staggered in and cursed and swore,
Maddened by the damning drink,
Verging on the very brink
Of delirium's fearful craze,
Scorched by hell's devouring blaze.
Oh, the sadness of her lot!
Father was a drunken sot.

Often in the village street,
Other children did she meet,
Who, with scorn and lips a-curl,
Said she was a drunkard's girl;
Sneeringly her person viewed,
Passed her by with manners rude;
And her life was sad and lone
Not a friend to call her own;
None to cheer her dreary heart,
From the world she walked apart.
Oh, the grief of little Dot!
Offspring of a drunken sot.

Nothing of a Savior's love,
Nothing of a home above,
Nothing of the path that leads,
Where the soul on manna feeds;

Nothing of the treasure bought
By the Savior, was she taught.
Mother, duty had forgot,
Father, wrecked, degraded sot.

When to womanhood she grew,
Phantom castles met her view,
Floating gaily in the air,
Painted all so bright and fair.
None to guide her tender feet,
In the path of virtue sweet;
Pressing on with eager mind,
To the coming danger blind;
Knowing not the tempter's wiles,
All bewildered with his smiles,
Till entangled in his net
All her hopes in darkness set,
And her sun went down in night
Void of faintest ray of light.
Short the sunny hour that shined
Then a drunkard's wife she pined,
Till in death her spirit fled,
And she slumbered with the dead.
Who can paint the mournful lot
Of the poor misguided Dot?

In her childhood's opening day,
Darkness brooding o'er her way;
Of a mother's care bereft,
To her own strange fancies left;
Like a trampled, broken flower,
Robbed of all its fragrant power,
All its beauty quite decayed,
Withered by some upas shade;
Only one brief hour of light
Closing in with darkest night;

Mother heedless of her child,
Father led by passions wild,
Husband, too, a drunken sot;
Oh! how sad the fate of Dot!

The Sweets of Love.

Oh! what is life where love is not?
    A dreary winter bleak and cold;
Where'er our pathway, what our lot,
    Love paints the landscape all with gold.

It speeds the hours on wings of light,
    And scatters roses in the way,
Illumes the darkest hours of night,
    And makes of life a summer day.

There is a love from heaven, divine,
    That binds the heart of man to God,
And makes his path with glory shine,
    And sheds its sunlight all abroad.

Why seek the empty things of earth,
    Which lure awhile then fade away?
Give me the joy of heavenly birth—
    Love's joy that never doth decay.

Oh, foretaste sweet of that above!
    Earnest of heaven's diviner ray,
When all the soul is bathed in love,
    And every cloud has flown away!

Unkind Words.

Oh, the words unkindly spoken!—
    How they pierce like adder's sting!
Oh, the friendships they have broken!
    Oh, the sorrows that they bring!

Causing wounds that smart and fester,
  Leaving ugly scars behind,
Scattering social joys that cluster
  Round the fireside to the wind.

Would to God we might recall them,
  But our beck is all in vain;
Would that something might befall them
  That they never rise again.

Tears may start and lips may quiver,
  Words can never be unsaid,
But their influence widens ever,
  O'er the living and the dead.

Saviour manifest thy kindness,
  Cover with thy precious blood
Words we uttered in our blindness
  When our hearts were far from God.

Fill us with thy loving spirit,
  Touch our lips with sacred fire,
Purge our tongues—we plead thy merit—
  Let thy love our hearts inspire.

Look to Jesus.

When on the deep waters of life's troubled ocean
  Thy vessel is tossed by the waves' foaming crest,
Oh! heed not the noise of the wild wind's commotion,
  But listen to Jesus, he'll tell thee of rest.

And fear not the rage of the wide heaving billow;
  The storm will subside at the Savior's behest:
Though seeming to sleep, he will rise from his pillow
  And calm the wild tempest to silence and rest.

When mists and dark clouds gather thick on thy heaven,
  And fades the last glimmer of day in the west,
He'll scatter the darkness, the clouds will be riven,
  And the charm of his presence will bring thee sweet rest.

And when thou art weary and worn with thy rowing,
  When nature exhausted would sink down to rest,
His tender compassion for thee overflowing,
  Will press thee to pillow thy head on his breast.

And shouldst thou be burdened with anguish and sorrow,
  Go take him thy burden, he'll give thee his rest:
Thy voyage will be short, at the dawn of the morrow
  Thy bark will be moored in the port of the blest.

A Mother's Lamentation.

Alas! the dear boy that so fondly I pressed
  Close to my heart in the years that are gone,
Nestling his little head down on my breast;
  Why have my fondest hopes vanished so soon?

Once I had fancied to see him grow strong—
  Strong in his manhood—for virtue and truth,
Loving the right and detesting the wrong:
  Now is he wrecked in the midst of his youth!

Would I had folded his little soft hands,
  Cold on his bosom in death's still embrace,
Yielded his form to the grave's icy bands,
  Looked the last time on his innocent face.

While in the midst of his boyhood days,
  Ere he had tasted the poisonous dram,
Wildered by passion's dark, devious ways,
  Lured by the goblet that sparkles to damn.

O, my poor child! thou art caught in the snare,
  The net of the fowler entangles thy feet;

Helpless as Samson when shorn of his hair;
   Scorned by thy captors, thy ruin complete.

Must thou in darkness and ruin descend
   Down to the depths of dishonor and woe?
Oh! my heart trembles to think of the end,
   When in a drunkard's grave thou art laid low.

If they had ruined this casket of clay;
   If they had robbed thee of silver and gold;
Had they but taken thy fair name away,
   Multiplied sorrows of earth many fold;

Yet had they left thee some hope of that peace
   Where the glad years of eternity roll;
But they have made every glimmer to cease;
   Yea, they have fiendishly murdered thy soul.

Life Transient.

Life is but a flitting shadow
   Passing by and gone so soon;
Like the firefly of the meadow
   In the misty nights of June;

Like the river swiftly gliding
   From the upland to the sea;
Ever changing, unabiding,
   Hasting to eternity.

As the vapor of the morning,
   Fading in the sun's bright ray;
Like the flower the fields adorning,
   Shortly drooping to decay.

As the tender grass that groweth
   In the verdant fields to-day,
Which tomorrow only knoweth
   As the mown and withered hay.

Like the meteor swiftly glancing
 Out across yon starry dome;
Like the wavelet playing, dancing,
 Breaking into spray and foam.

As the rainbow of the heaven
 Only knows a transient stay;
As the rosy blush of even
 In the darkness fades away,

So is life: man only lingers
 Briefly in his earthly home;
Cruel Death with icy fingers
 Soon conveys him to the tomb.

Though so brief life's mingled story,
 Yet how wondrous is its trend!
Leading to a life of glory,
 On to joys that never end;

Or as wilful man may guide it,
 Heedless of the beckoning light,
In the path where sins betide it,
 Leading down to endless night.

There Shall Be No Night There.—Rev. 22:5.

Here night and darkness on our sky,
 When sins beset us, gather fast,
Till light from heaven illumes our eye,
 And bids the shadows hasten past.
But in yon world so bright and fair,
 Darkness and night shall never come;
No sin shall ever enter there,
 Nor sorrow cast one shade of gloom.

Here cruel Death on tireless wings
　　Hovers in darkness o'er the way,
His shadow on our pathway flings
　　And dims our every earthly ray.
But funeral rite and dirge and pall
　　Shall never mar heaven's glorious day;
No fear of death shall ever fall,
　　To make one single joy decay.

Here clouds of error, dense, profound,
　　Obscure fair Reason's glimmering light,
And mists and darkness gather round,
　　Shrouding the soul in mental night.
But as we're seen there we shall see;
　　There we shall know as we are known;
Unfading glory there shall be
　　The heritage of every one.

Invitation to The Young.

Come in the spring-time of life's fleeting day,
Come while all nature looks cheerful and gay,
Come ere deep sorrows have furrowed your brow;
Come to the Saviour, oh! come to him now.

In the dim future thine eye cannot see
All of the pain that thy portion may be,
All of the anguish and all of the night:
Come to the Saviour he'll guide thee aright.

Oft on thy journey thou surely will meet
Snares to entangle thine unwary feet,
Set by the temper to lure thee astray:
'Come, let the Saviour enlighten thy way.

Hope will deceive you while sorrows pursue;
Friends may desert you, but Jesus is true
Come, give unto him a warm, loving heart;
Come, let your Saviour his blessing impart.

Come, for in love he is calling for thee;
Wait not one moment, but hasten thy plea;
Seek for thy pardon and utter thy vow;
Come to the Saviour, oh! come to him now.

To The Middle Aged.

You who have waited till life's middle prime,
Halted and lingered and sported with time,
Mocked by the visions that rose on your view;
Come to the Saviour, he's waiting for you.

When you look back on the years that have flown,
On the bright dreams that have faded and gone,
On the brief pleasures that earth can afford,
Why will you turn from your Saviour and Lord?

Surely the joys of the past should suffice,
Sinking and dying as soon as they rise;
Jesus now offers you joys that endure
Long as eternity, fadeless and pure.

Lo! in the garden he suffered for thee,
Mocked by the soldiers, he died on the tree;
Hid was the face of the Father; alone
He suffered deep anguish thy sins to atone.

Think of the sorrow, the anguish, the pain;
Give him the vigor and strength that remain,
Give him the years that are passing away:
Come, he invites you, oh! come while you may.

To The Aged.

You who are nearing the shadows of night,
Anxiously watching the fast-fading light
Come ere the daylight forever is gone;
Come, and the Saviour will make you his own.

Though thou are nearing the end of the race,
Yet if he beckons there's hope in thy case;
Though thou hast robbed him he loves even thee:
Come, for his grace is abundant and free.

Though thou hast wandered afar from the fold,
On the bleak mountains so dreary and cold,
Out on the desert so cheerless and bare,
Yet he has watched thee with tenderest care.

Though in your crown there may glitter no star,
Yet there'll be nothing your pleasure to mar;
Oh! 'twill be glorious your Saviour to meet,
Glorious to fall at his nail-wounded feet.

Come ere the darkness envelopes you round;
Come while forgiveness and rest may be found;
Come ere you sink to remediless doom
Come while he calls you, oh! hasten and come.

Musings On Picket.

Standing on picket down by the thicket,
    Looking out into the dark misty night;
Body all weary and soul sad and dreary,
    Longing and waiting for morn's blessed light.

Bosom still smarting because of the parting
    From those that were dear by affection's strong tie,
When the tear started as they, the true-hearted,
    Tenderly whispered the parting good by.

What of the morrow? disaster and sorrow,
    Vict'ry and triumph, oh! which shall it be?
Say, shall we falter? No, on the altar,
    Country, we conquer, or perish for thee.

O Lord! o'er the battle, mid tumult and rattle,
    Stretch out in mercy the arm of thy might:
Be our salvation; preserve us a nation;
    Scatter the traitors and succor the right.

Long has oppression by wrong and transgression
    Crushed out the hope of the poor toiling slave:
With his heart bleeding to thee he is pleading;
    God of the universe, listen and save.

Star of the Morning, in beauty adorning
    All that thou risest on, bid the night flee;
Hasten the springing of brighter days, bringing
    Peace upon earth and devotion to thee.

Alexander and Rosalind.

HE.

Sweet Rosalind, my darling girl,
    You know I love you dearly:
But why upon your lips that curl?
    I am not joking merely;
But I would gladly make you mine:
    Oh! come no longer dally,
Why does your heart to fear incline?
    Pray, make its courage rally.

SHE.

Why, Alexander, I'm afraid
    That when our courtship's ended,
And I no more a blushing maid,
    Your love will be suspended:
For many months ago I guessed
    Your love was quite divided;
And which of two you love the best
    You still are undecided.

HE.

O Rosalind! my heart is true,
    Pray why this harsh reflection?
For never other lass than you
    Can win my heart's affection:
I see you nightly in my dreams
    With ways so sweet and cheery,
This world without your presence seems
    A desert lone and dreary.

SHE.

But, Alexander, don't you know
    That love is oft self-seeing?
'Tis selfishness that makes it glow—
    It's truth that I am speaking—
And should the one you love require
    Of you some self-denial,
How soon would die love's waving fire
    All smothered by such trial!

HE.

Dear Rosalind, my very life
    I'd lay down at your pleasure;
And could I now but call you wife
    My joy would know no measure;
And I would gladly sacrifice
    Your every task to lighten,
And every power that in me lies
    Employ your path to brighten.

SHE.

'Tis not the love of other maid
    Of which I am complaining;
Of other lass I'm not afraid,
    But what your lips is staining;

I fear you love the poison weed
    With love still growing stronger;
And were you true to me indeed,
    How could you love it longer?

I've asked you oft to lay it by;
    It shocks my sense of neatness;
And though you chew it on the sly,
    Your breath has lost its sweetness:
And when the honey moon is passed,
    The novelty all over,
I fear that you will prove at last
    A faithless, fickle lover.

For, if you cannot conquer now
    When full of youthful ardor,
If you've no strength to keep your vow,
    In age you'll find it harder.
I'll settle this affair today;
    I feel my courage rally;
I will not wed; "I say thee nay;"
    I will no longer dally.

To The South Wind.

Balmy Wind, from sunny South,
    Softly kissing brow and cheek,
Words of gladness fill our mouth
    When of thee our lips would speak.

Winter comes with sullen frown,
    Fills the air with icy breath,
Turns the smiling verdure brown,
    Spreads o'er earth the robes of death;

Bids the wailing tempest blow
    Through the cold and cheerless night,

Driving clouds of blinding snow,
   Hiding moon and stars from sight;

Bids the merry dancing brooks
   Babbling by in summertide,
Singing to the trees and rocks,
   Under icy covers hide.

Happy songsters sing no more
   In the sighing, leafless trees;
Humming insects cease to pour
   Dreamy music on the breeze.

Fragrant breath of opening flowers
   Greets no more our ravished sense;
Neath the snow their slumbering powers
   Rest till spring shall call them thence.

Flocks and herds no more we see
   Grazing in the pastures green,
Lying neath the shady tree,
   Resting, happy and serene.

Winter has his task to do,
   And performs his labor well;
But his stern and sullen brow
   Fiercely lowers like demon fell.

And we dread his savage mien
   Though we know he comes to bless;
Though severe his cheerless reign,
   Yet we would not bid it cease.

Still when gentle spring returns,
   And thy whisperings soft we hear,
Life anew within us burns,
   Bringing buoyant hope and cheer.

Those by poverty oppressed,
   Longing o'er their meager fare,

Sorely burdened and distressed
    With their crushing load of care,

Greet thee with a welcome smile,
    Feel fresh hope within them glow,
Drop their broodings for the while,
    When they feel thy genial flow,

From the sunny fields afar
    On thy journey thou hast sped,
Bearing perfumes rich and rare
    By unfolding nature shed.

Thou hast breathed upon the sick
    Pining on his bed of pain,
Softly fanned the glowing cheek
    Of the merry lass and swain.

Like thy Maker thou dost bring
    Blessings to the good and bad,
All along thy pathway fling
    Greetings to the gay and sad.

As thy Maker tempers thee,
    Sending thee the world to bless,
May his spirit work in me,
    Banishing all selfishness;

Bidding me in love go forth,
    Bearing blessings as I go,
As thy soft breath cheers the North,
    Driving thence the frost and snow.

Song Of The Wind.

The wind from northern zone was chill,
Its icy breathings seemed to thrill
My soul with dread; through shrub and tree
It piped its mournful melody;

To faded flower and withered grass
Sang solemn dirges in its pass;
Sighed mid the brown and wrinkled leaves,
And wailed along the cottage eaves;
To gable cornice made its moan
In accents sad with varying tone.

I listened to each mournful strain,
While to my mind the sad refrain
 Brought back the memory of the years,
Freighted with good, mingled with tears,
Which o'er my wayward life had flown;
And as I, musing, sat alone,
I saw a hand divine and strong
Had led me all the way along;
And as God's goodness passed before,
I could but worship and adore.

And then the wild wind seemed to say,
Murmur no more at Time's brief stay;
You in your blindness failed to see
God's purposes in Time and me;
But listen while to you I sing
Of blessings which to man we bring,
And how unlike and like are we
In working out man's destiny.

We linger, neither I nor Time;
I hasten on to fairer clime,
To sunny South's warm verdant fields;
 So Time goes by on rapid wheels,
Bearing his freight of deathless souls
To where eternal day unfolds.
Alike in this are Time and I,
Time lingers not, I swiftly fly;
fickled all my flight shall be,
while onward to eternity

Time presses in its rapid flight,
As wing the fleeting day and night.

I sing the requiems of the dead,
Bemoan the summer glories fled;
But, silent as yon starry spheres,
Time onward moves through all the years.
Though at our dealings man repines,
We both fulfill God's great designs;
Each in his own peculiar way
Performs his mission of today;
And when tomorrow comes we still
Shall feel the impulse of his will;
Obedient each to his behest,
We weary not nor seek for rest.

Of my own mission let me tell,
How I perform my labor well;
Then will I sing the task sublime
Fulfilled by ceaseless, silent Time.

I come with soft and fragrant breath,
When earth revives from winter's death,
To help the sunshine and the showers
Awaken nature's slumbering powers,
To bid the grass its life renew
Sweet flower unfold with brilliant hue,
The groves put on their robes of green,
The landscap glow with smiling sheen,
While birds pour out in gladsome notes
Their songs of love from warbling throats,
And happy insects gaily sing,
Gliding through air on flashing wing,
And by the streams in noisy glee
Reptiles breath out their melody.

When summer comes with lengthened days,
And Sol shoots down his burning rays,

I fan the weary laborer's cheek,
Revive his strength when worn and weak;
At close of day in cooling breeze
I come from mountain height and seas;
I bring the clouds that pour the rain
On thirsty grass and drooping grain,
Causing the herbage to revive
And sun-scorched vegetation live.

And when the passing year grows old
I harden man for winter's cold,
Impart fresh vigor to his frame,
To glowing life a brighter flame,
Till he can meet the rigors wild
Of winter with a welcome smile.

Though sometimes with resistless might
I crush man in my rapid flight,
Yet blessing s rich to him I bring
As to and fro my way I wing.
I drive away the vapors foul
 Which rise from stagnant marsh and pool,
Dispell the poison in the air,
Drive it to desert wilds afar
Or where old noisy Ocean raves
And swallows it beneath his waves.

Brought back the memory of the years,
Freighted with good, mingled with tears
Which o'er my wayward life had flown;
And as I, musing, sat alone,
 I saw a hand divine and strong,
 Had led me all the way along;
 And as God's goodness passed before
I could but worship and adore.

And then the wild wind seemed to say,
Murmur no more at Time's brief stay;

You in your blindness failed to see
God's purposes in Time and me;
But listen while to you I sing
Of blessings which to man we bring,
And how unlike and like are we
In working out man's destiny.

We linger, neither I nor Time;
I hasten on to fairer clime,
To sunny South's warm verdant fields;
So Time goes by on rapid wheels,
Bearing his freight of deathless souls
To where eternal day unfolds.
Alike in this are time and I—
Time lingers not, I swiftly fly;
But fickled all my flight shall be,
While onward to eternity
Time presses in its rapid flight,
As wing the fleeting day and night.

I sing the requiems of the dead,
Bemoan the summer glories fled;
But, silent as yon starry spheres,
Time onward moves through all the years.
Though at our dealings man repines,
We both fulfill God's great designs;
Each in his own peculiar way
Performs his mission of to-day;
And when to-morrow comes we still
Shall feel the impulse of his will;
Obedient each to his behest,
We weary not nor seek for rest.

Of my own mission let me tell,
How I perform my labors well;
Then will I sing the task sublime,
Fulfilled by ceaseless, silent Time.

I come with soft and fragrant breath,
When earth revives from Winter's death,
To help the sunshine and the showers
Awaken Nature's slumbering powers;
To bid the grass its life renew,
 Sweet flower unfold with brilliant hue,
The groves put on their robes of green,
 The landscape glow with smiling sheen,
While birds pour out in gladsome notes
Their songs of love from warbling throats,
And happy insects gaily sing,
Gliding through air on flashing wing,
And by the streams in noisy glee
Reptiles breathe out their melody.

When Summer comes with lengthened days,
 And Sol shoots down his burning rays,
I fan the weary laborer's cheek,
Revive his strength when worn and weak:
At close of day in cooling breeze
I come from mountain height and seas;
I bring the clouds that pour the rain
On thirsty grass and drooping grain,
Causing the herbage to revive
And sun-scorched vegetation live.

And when the passing year grows old,
I harden man for Winter's cold,
Impart fresh vigor to his frame,
To glowing life a brighter flame,
Till he can meet the rigors wild
Of Winter with a welcome smile.

Though sometimes with resistless might
I crush man in my rapid flight;
Yet blessings rich to him I bring
As to and fro my way I wing;
I drive away the vapors foul

Which rise from stagnant marsh and pool,
Dispel the poison in the air,
Drive it to desert wilds afar,
Or where old noisy Ocean raves
And swallows it beneath its waves.

Though great my might, man chains me still
And makes me subject to his will:
I waft the hardy mariner
In gallant ship to climes afar;
I drive the pump that lifts the draught
By man and other creatures sought,
And make the busy wheel go round
Where food for man and beast is ground;
In many ways I render aid,
Nor murmur at my task unpaid;
Across the land, across the deep,
Though man may rest I onward sweep,
And only halt at God's command,
Who holds me in his powerful hand.

Time's Task.

Time brings the dawn of life's brief day,
Its balmy Spring, its smiling May,
With incense filling all the air,
Verdure and freshness everywhere;
Music that charms the listening ear,
Its cadence floating far and near;
The hour of gladness when the light
Is first revealed to infant's sight,—
Gladness to her whose agony
Brings life to one whose life may be;
If led in wisdom's pleasant ways,
To her a joy through all her days;
The fragrance of a mother's love,
Seeming like odors from above,

When to her fond and gentle breast
The infant form is softely prest
Love's tie as soft as silken strand
Binding like steel the household band;
The breathings of a parent's prayer,
A parent's hope, a parent's care.

And through the fast receding years
Time onward speeds till youth appears,
When things that held the infant mind
Like magic spell are left behind;
When toys and sports are laid aside,
The mind no longer occupied
With thoughts on childish pleasures bent,
Longing for some new wonderment,
On idle tales and simple plays
Which charmed so much the early days.

New thoughts and longings now arise,
Born of some influence from the skies;
The soul its worth begins to see,
And ponders o'er its destiny;
The mind approves God's holy law,
Its precepts just he reads with awe;
He sees his very being bent
To wrong and struggles to repent;
But while he strives he feels within
That law that ever prompts to sin,
And cries, "Oh, wretched man am I,
I fain would live, but still I die."

Eternity weighs on his heart;
What will its countless years impart?
What lies beyond the bounds of time,
Anguish or joy in yonder clime?
At thoughts of death the mind recoils;
Death's shadow all his pleasure spoils;

Conscience her lash with vigor plies,
The spirit sinks, the weeping eyes
Turned toward the victim on the tree,
Bleeding to set the captive free;
The heart relents the stubborn will
Breaks down and 'neath the rod holds still,
Till Jesus speaks with cheering voice:
"I loose thy bands, arise, rejoice;
Thy sins, though great, are all forgiven;
I now appoint thee heir of heaven:
I died for thee; for me to live
Be all thy joy; I freely give
The strength thy weakness shall require;
I'll fill thine every pure desire,
And bring thee calm when cares oppress,
Relief in sorrow and distress;
Then after life's short race is run,
The struggle o'er, the battle won,
I'll bid thee lay thine armor down,
And deck thy head with starry crown."

The tear-dimmed eyes in faith look up;
The breast expands with new-born hope;
The spirit strong in God's own might,
Now clad in heavenly armor bright,
Heedless of else, for glory starts,
From every earthly idol parts,
Presses the path where Jesus leads,
Though Satan oft His march impedes.
His eye is fixed upon the goal
Where lies the prize; his ravished soul
Has visions of the rich estate—
The home beyond the pearly gate—
Prepared for those who toil and fight
Against the wrong, for truth and right.

He hungers now for righteousness,
Adores his Maker, seeks to bless

Poor blinded travelers to the grave,
Points to the sky and warns the slave
Of sin to turn from error's path,
Seek shelter from Jehovah's wrath
In Jesus' wounds, and there abide
And cleans him in the healing tide,
Till he appear in glorious dress—
Unspotted robes of holiness.

But time halts not for good or ill,
For youth or age, but ownward still
Hurries the pilgrim down to death,
Which withers with its chilling breath
The mortal frame, closes this scene
And lifts the veil that hangs between
This life and that which lies before,
Where things of earth beset no more.

As man looks back along the road
That his bewildered feet have trod,
Life's verdant spring, its summer rays,
It's autumn chill, it's winter days,
Its rosy dawn and sunny noon,
Its winged moments, gone so soon,
Its years that glided by so fast,
Seem all like phantoms of the past.

And yet life is a glorious thing,
A deathless germ, from it may spring
A nobler life whose fervent glow
Knows naught of winter's ice and snow,
Of setting sun and gathering shade;
Whose springtime beauties never fade;
A life that endless joy begets,
Where naught of sorrow e'er besets,
That through the endless years flows on,
More radiant than the noonday sun.

Then why repine at Time's swift flight?
Why dread the shades of death's dark night?
If thou hast walked as God designed,
Cherished a pure and heavenly mind;
If thou hast turned away thy face
From every idol, if no place
For sin within thy breast is found,
If by Christ's law thy soul is bound
And thou art following holiness,
In heaven thou soon wilt find thy place.

This is the way that God has planned
To people yonder happy land:
The infant spirit finds its birth
Here in this lower vale of earth;
Is led along the slippery road,
Held by the tender hand of God,
Is pointed to the narrow way
That leads to life, the Spirit's ray
 Illumes the chart to mortals given
To guide their footsteps on to heaven;
And he who runs this heavenly race
Finds strength in Christ's abounding grace;
Time bears him on with rapid flight
Till heaven bursts on his ravished sight.

Good-bye you'll hear my voice again,
Perhaps in softer, sweeter strain,
And, as I ever God obey,
Go on thyself in his own way.

The Disconsolate.

One who had wandered sat weeping in sadness,
    Swayed was her spirit like reeds in the wind:
I said all the world is rejoicing in gladness,
    I pray leave your sin and your sorrow behind.

"Oh how can I leave them!" she answered in anguish,
  "How from this bondage that holds me be free?
In the strong fetters of habit I languish,
  And the wide world has no solace for me.

"Once in my sorrow I turned to the Savior,
  Sought by repentance to make him my own,
Earnestly strove to amend my behavior,
  Wearily struggled in weakness alone.

"Trembling I turned to my sisters with pleading,
  Asked for the aid that their hands might afford:
Some looked in pity, their tender hearts bleeding;
  But they could utter no comforting word.

"Others beheld me with sneers and with scorning,
  Turned from beholding with haughty disdain:
How my heart sank as I heard the stern warning
  Never to enter their presence again.

"Sweetly they beam on my partner in sinning,
  Knowing full well that he led me astray;
And their bright smiles he is constantly winning;
  But from his victim their eyes turn away.

"Onward I hasten, down deeper and deeper;
  Yet I would gladly return from my ways;
As I press onward the pathway grows steeper
  Downward, and nothing my wayward feet stays."

Mary's Dream.

The shadows had gathered, the toils of the day
  Were ended, and faint on her hard scanty bed,
With spirit dejected, her weary form lay;
  No plans for to-morrow; ambition was dead.

But mem'ry was busy with scenes of the past,
   Ere rum had invaded her once-happy home
And made of her bosom a desolate waste,
   A dreary Sahara, no verdure nor bloom.

But nature soon triumphed—she slept; and she dreamed
   That she was a child again; bright to her view,
The scenes once enacted arose and it seemed
   That childhood was leading its pleasures anew.

The home of her girlhood was hers with its charms,
   And the tide of her joy in her bosom ran high;
She felt the embrace of a fond mother's arms,
   And caught the sweet light of her love-beaming eye.

Once more on the knee of her father she sat,
   And prest her soft lips in a kiss on his face,
Delighted his ear with her innocent chat,
   Encircled his neck with a child's warm embrace.

With brother and sister she sported again
   Upon the green sward 'neath the wide-spreading tree
And down by the brook where the bright waters ran
   Amid the wild tangle that skirted the lea;

And down in the dell where the wild berries grew,
   And over the hill by the rock-sheltered cove,
And up by the ledge where the eve-swallows flew
   With burdens of clay in their labors of love.

She knelt once again at the family shrine,
   And joined in the hymns of the bright "long ago,"
And felt in her bosom the impulse devine
   That made her glad spirit with joy overflow.

She dreamed of the time when she yielded her all
   To Jesus and laid down her life at his feet,
And willingly heeding the Spirit's sweet call,
   She drank of life's river, her pleasure complete.

She looked in the eyes of the youth that had wooed
    And won her young heart with a lover's sweet guile;
Again at the altar of Hymen she stood,
    And felt she was basking in heaven's own smile.

The words that united were checked in their course,
    The voice of the maniac rung in her ear
With tones indistinct but savage and hoarse,
    Which brought her from dream-land half palsied with
        fear.

How bright was the vision! how short was its stay!
    The morrow brought only deep sorrow and gloom;
Of hope through the darkness she saw not a ray,
    Save only the light through gates of the tomb.

The heart she had trusted had hardened to stone,
    And all its warm impulses sunk to decay;
The human had vanished, the beastly alone
    Held over its throbbings a limitless sway.

The Inebriate's Soliloquy.

How long have I struggled to sever the chain
That holds me in bondage! I struggle in vain;
The master that binds me to service so base,
But mocks at my efforts and laughs in my face.

I turn to my kindred and long for the aid
That sympathy offers; they only upbraid.
The wife of my bosom alone seems to know
And tenderly feel for my anguish and woe.

My little ones look with their eyes staring wide,
And fearful of danger, they flee from my side;
    And the gap that divides us grows broader each day,
    And the love, once so warm, is fast fading away.

The neighbors who greeted me once with a smile
And a hearty hand-shake and a word of good will,
Now eye me askance with a look of disdain,
But they know not the depth of my soul's bitter pain.

They say I should turn from my cups and amend;
But the grasp of the giant with which I contend,
Unyielding as iron, holds fast to my hand,
And hurries me onward, though fain I would stand.

Yes, fain would I halt in my rapid descent;
But vain are my efforts, in vain I relent
The follies that took all my manhood away,
And left me a victim to passion's wild play.

Oh! how can I halt when the tempter displays
His wares to my senses, my being ablaze
With passion's fierce burning that knows no control
And only is sated by rum's fiery bowl?

I walk in the street, and the reveler's song,
As borne on the night air, comes floating along,
And odors are wafted that waken desire,
And my purposes vanish like lint in the fire.

Oh! would they were gone, for I cannot say nay;
These dens of temptation that lure me astray.
Ye servants of Jesus, I pray lend a hand,
And banish forever these dens from the land.

So Much to Please.

I saw low in the east the morning light
    Painting the sky and climbing up the steep,
'Till all aglow was seen the vaulted height
    Smiling on earth, emerging from its sleep.

I heard the mingled notes of mockingbird,
    The chatter of the sparrow in the tree,

The rustle of the leaves by soft wind stirred,
    The busy hum of honey-culling bee.

I saw the flash of insect's gilded wing,
    As up and down it darted here and there,
And heard the song that other creatures sing,
    Filling with music all the ambient air.

Beheld the sun advancing up the sky,
    And the broad landscape glowing in its ray,
The ripening grains nod to the passer-by—
    A cheery greeting, at the opening day.

I saw the housewife at her morning task
    Buoyant with hope, her features all aglow,
Seeming like one whose soul was wont to bask
    In heaven's own light, borne up from all below.

The ceaseless rumble and the click of steel,
    Rising from mill and field's yellow grain,
Sounded afar as turned the mighty wheel
    Of human labor with unflagging main.

I saw the day advance and then decline,
    The sun go down amid the golden haze,
The radiant sky in wonderous beauty shine,
    The straying clouds reflect the evening rays,

And then the chirp of merry insects fell
    Upon my grateful ear, and the soft hum
Of sentient creatures, like some magic spell,
    Bound all my being till my lips were dumb.

I saw the shadows creeping o'er the earth.
    The stars grow bright to cheer the coming gloom,
The household fondly gather round the hearth,—
    Type of that blissful gathering yet to come.

Then songs of praise went up like incense sweet,
    Fragrant with humble love and holy joy,
And pleadings strong for heavenly grace to meet
    The wiles of sin and all its power destroy.

The pleasing scenes that daily meet the eye,
  The sounds that fall upon the listening ear,
Add wings to the glad hours that swiftly fly,
  And brighten all the moments of the year.

The springtime comes with magic undefined—
  A charm that words are powerless to express;
A nameless something permeates the mind,
  And clothes its every thought with radiant dress.

The glowing summer paints each vale and hill
  With varying tints of every smiling hue;
And nature makes the grateful senses thrill
  With pleasures that are ever bright and new.

The forest in autumnal robes arrayed,
  The ripening fruit exhaling on the air
Its fragrance rich, the perfume of the glade,
  Bring joys that prince and beggar both may share.

And even winter in its furious rage,
  When storm clouds sweep in anger o'er the sky,
And furious winds their utmost power engage
  To pile the gathering snowdrifts broad and high.

Has charms for him who loves the grand, sublime,
  Whose eye beholds in nature's ever varying mood
Something on which to feast, nor spends his time
  In sinful murmurings at the hand of God.

Oh! there is much to make man happy here—
  The joys of sense, the pleasures of the mind,
And social ties that bind to kindred dear,
  And radiant hope by heavenly grace refined.

If selfishness would cease to hold the rein
  Man might walk forth in perfect liberty;
Oh! were it not for sin's dark, deadly bane,
  This earth a blissful Eden still would be.

CONTENTS.

CPSIA information can be obtained
at www.ICGtesting.com
Printed in the USA
BVHW042052160223
658667BV00006B/894